Advance Praise for *These are Love(d) Letters*

"Like many poets and readers of my generation, I value letters as a kind of sacred interstice in which conversation and collaboration become finessed by the gravity of time and the interruption or enabling of the most romantic of government subsidiaries: the post office. It is no small task, but Hawkins acts as a sort of Virgil through the various levels of *These are Love(d) Letters*—theoretical, figurative, projective, and personal—so that we, as readers, are never left alone with these letters, nor with the question of what they might mean. This guidance, as well as the author's smart vulnerability, is a great generosity and one that threads itself throughout. This book will stay with me for a long time."

—Meg Day, author of *Last Psalm at Sea Level*

"Ames Hawkins renders the inheritance of a parent's love letters into a queer palimpsest of legacy, knowledge, and experience. Letters as collections. Letters as raw theory. Letters as family tracings. Letters as identity archive. This book is essay art at its most exquisite, a brilliant new standard for artifact-based nonfiction."

—Barrie Jean Borich, author of *Apocalypse, Darling*, and *Body Geographic*

"Hybrid, multiform, queer, and truly polyphonic, Ames Hawkins's *These are Love(d) Letters* recollects her enigmatic gay father through a packet of love letters that he wrote to her mother. Curious bequeathings, the ecology of stamps, and a history of companion texts drawn from a larger literary archive of queer love-making through letters form the backdrop to this book's foremost aim: 'how to transport yourself and others toward bliss.' The combination of Hawkins's lucid prose and Jessica Jacobs's inspired design set a new bar for critical-creative writing and cross-over art. An immensely stirring and utterly unpredictable book."

—Mary Cappello, author of *Life Breaks In: A Mood Almanack*

"In a work both academic and intimate, Ames Hawkins charts the materiality of desire in the written word, the body of the letter, and the body of the beloved. Hawkins invites the reader along on a lyric exploration of love, the process of 'mak[ing] sacred what would otherwise be random.'"

—Valerie Wetlaufer, author of *Mysterious Acts by My People*

These
are
love (d)
Letters

3/24/22

Dear Trent,

From one Michigander
to another: So good to
meet you. Keep writing
no matter what. From our
hands to yours.

xo
Ames

NOWHERELAND
1966
2019

These are *love*(d) Letters

AMES HAWKINS

Designed by Jessica Jacobs

 WAYNE STATE UNIVERSITY PRESS
Detroit

Made in Michigan Writers Series
General Editors
Michael Delp, Interlochen Center for the Arts
M. L. Liebler, Wayne State University

ISBN 978–0-8143-4726-3 (paperback)
ISBN 978–0-8143-4727-0 (ebook)
Library of Congress Control Number: 2019938100

Publication of this book was made possible by a generous gift from The Meijer Foundation. This work is supported in part by an award from the Michigan Council for Arts and Cultural Affairs.

michigan
council for
&arts
cultural
affairs

Wayne State University Press
Leonard N. Simons Building
4809 Woodward Avenue
Detroit, Michigan 48201–1309
Visit us online at wsupress.wayne.edu

To my mother, Patricia Eileen O'Brien:

For gifting me the letters.
For trusting me with the writing of this book.

Air Mail
VOORHEESVILLE, N.Y. AUG 30 PM 1966 12186
5¢ U.S. POSTAGE
5¢ U.S. POSTAGE
Miss Patricia O'Brien
University of Michigan
722 South Forest
Ann Arbor, Michigan
Hawkins, RD#1 Voorheesville, New York — 12186

It is a simple act when my mother gives me the letters.

Air Mail
VOORHEESVILLE AUG 30 PM 1966 N.Y. 12186
5c U.S. POSTAGE
Miss Patricia O'Brien
University of Michigan
922 South Forest
Ann Arbor, Michigan
Buffalo, N.Y.-14216
National

She hands them to me across the drop-leaf table, the one that sits in front of the couch that sits in the living room in the house that she has, by this time, lived in nearly twice as many years as we all lived together on Whittier Road, the place where we made and unmade our nuclear family.

She hands me the letters because they are hers to give, these twenty missives sent to her by my father, twenty letters he consciously crafted to woo her, twenty pieces of mail postmarked between August 30 and October 4, 1966. Twenty epistles she kept for over forty years. She says she read them all one final time and now gives them to me because I am writing about my father, about sexuality, about art, about his diagnosis of advanced AIDS.

She hands me the letters and says she doesn't know why she kept them, other than perhaps to now be giving them to me. She hands me the letters, and time is so still I can barely hear it breathe. It stills and distills into recognition of this as an instance—similar to birth, death, graduation, marriage—that cleaves into halves my life: the time before knowing about the letters, and the time after she gives them to me.

I take the letters from her, count them, note the variety of the envelopes, the range of inks, the hand that I know to be my father's, put them into a large white Tyvek envelope, and don't touch them again for another year and a half.

In the first letter, the only one he ever types, my father begins with a poem by e.e. cummings: "love is the only ever god." I smile at this almost-twenty-two-year-old who invokes the classic love letter move, this reproduction of the words of another, offered to her as a way to get to know something about him. He admits that this letter is not his first attempt at writing. The one he "began last night" he "really didn't like." He cites poor handwriting as a reason for typing. Yet his "chicken scratches" become a perfectly acceptable form of communication from this point forward. Partly because of expediency. It is quicker to write by hand than to use the typewriter. But also because of the intimacy he feels in the grip of a pen, in the movement of his hand, in the lateness of the hour during which he often writes.

Upon first reading, this first letter doesn't seem very intimate. It's basic, fairly boring, and doesn't say all that much. There's an admitted state of confusion, a declaration of love. There's time, there's effort, and the framing of a shared world. There is writing. There are words. Words to which he directly refers. Both those they speak to one another on the phone and those he writes to her on this page. And yet.

Yet this love letter, though identifiable as a love letter, is also different. In addition to the poem, my father includes two small squares cut from paper maps. One is of a section of the Hudson Valley in New York, and the other a part of the coast of Connecticut. Other than a caption that reads, "nothing places now—but not long ago they had us and something . . . ," there is no direct reference to what happened there. Representations of the spaces my parents were in together at one time make clear at the moment of this writing they are no longer physically proximate. The distance between them is simultaneously reinforced and collapsed.

From these "nothing places," the people who will become my parents begin to craft their own story. From this NOWHERELAND, my father's letters open a space for a story that can be different. It is the distance that enables and empowers intimacy. It is an intimacy fueled by difference. Without knowing it, through these letters they begin to write the beginning of the rest of their lives.

love

I shall speak then of the letter *a*, the first letter which it seemed necessary to introduce now and then in writing the word *différance*. This seemed necessary in the course of writing about writing, and of writing within a writing whose different strokes all pass, in certain respects, through a gross spelling mistake, through violations of the rules governing writing, violating the law that governs writing and regulates its conventions of propriety. In fact, or theory, we can always erase or lessen this spelling mistake, and, in each case, while these are analytically different from one another but for practical purposes the same, find it grave, unseemly, or, indeed, supposing the greatest ingeniousness, amusing.

—Jacques Derrida, "Différance"

NOWHERELAND

Ciao,

Found this last night and I liked it when I first read it a few years back:

nothing places now--but not long ago they had us
and something........

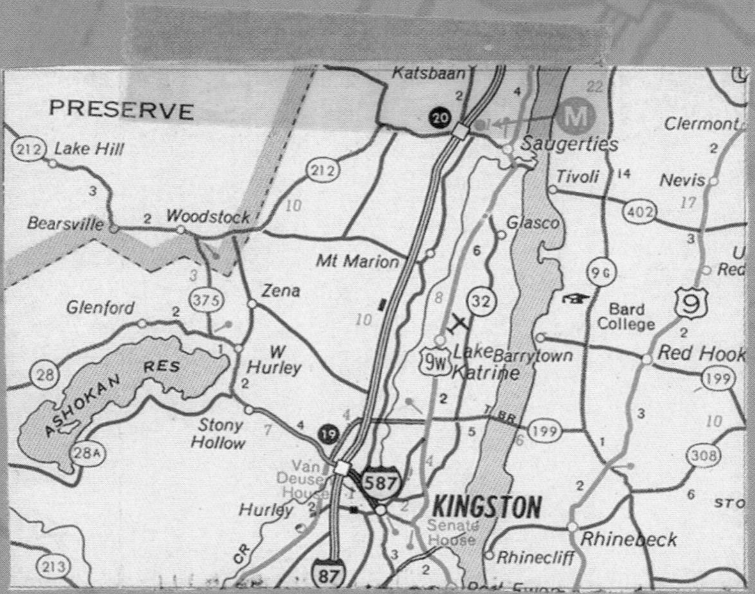

Katsbaan
PRESERVE
Saugerties
Clermont
Lake Hill
Tivoli
Nevis
Woodstock
Bearsville
Glasco
Mt Marion
Zena
Red Hook
Glenford
Bard College
W Hurley
Lake Katrine
Barrytown
ASHOKAN RES
Stony Hollow
Van Deuse House
KINGSTON
Hurley
Senate House
Rhinebeck
Rhinecliff

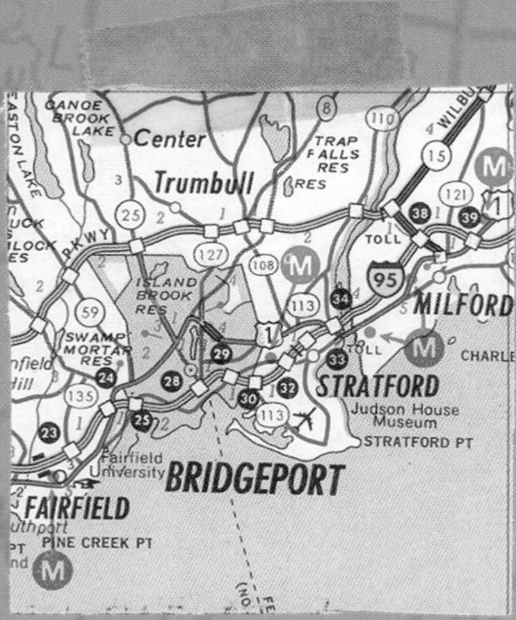

CANOE BROOK LAKE
Center
Trumbull
TRAP FALLS RES
EASTON LAKE
ISLAND BROOK RES
SWAMP MORTAR RES
TOLL
MILFORD
STRATFORD
Judson House Museum
STRATFORD PT
Fairfield University
BRIDGEPORT
FAIRFIELD
PINE CREEK PT

---- e.e. cummings, consummate White Anglo-Saxon Protestant Yankee who championed individualism and often condemned the role of the government, would have, despite his vocation as artist, been understood to be a model citizen from the Hawkins family perspective. I know it is likely that my father chose this poem somewhat randomly, having remembered it from some English class or even pulled it from a book on the occasion of writing to my mother what appears to be the first love letter. I imagine e.e. cummings as a kind of kindred spirit for my father, a representative of our American aristocracy who was both poet and painter, an artist with whom I am sure my father could identify, would have wanted to identify.

It would be absurd to create an aesthetic parallel between cummings and my father, and yet I see the similarities in their stories and sentiments, albeit in some kind of mirrored reverse. cummings rejected a child and saved every poem, every painting, every scrap of writing, all in the name of his art. My father remained in his marriage, with his children. He destroyed or somehow expelled, by fire, force, trash, robbery, or abandonment, nearly all he created. This, too, was all done in the name of art.

In the tales told about e.e. cummings and George Hawkins, men who cared most deeply, perhaps only, for their own art, we hear echoed *différance*.

nous sommes tres bien ensemble

In a coffeehouse in Ann Arbor, Michigan, forty-four years after the letters have been written, my mother admits to me that my father's artistic way of living—this art-life—this is what she had wanted, too.

love

In *The Art of Intimacy: The Space Between*, Stacey D'Erasmo begins with two questions: "What is the nature of intimacy, of what happens in the space between us? And how do we, as writers, catch or reflect it on the page?" Through her exploration of a range of twentieth- and twenty-first-century literature, D'Erasmo offers that intimacy is never built on the expected, on what is already anticipated and understood. Intimacy isn't created through stereotypes or expectations. Above all, the creation of intimacy in literature cannot be forced. D'Erasmo warns: "When we come to the page hoping to reveal something about intimacy, it is all too easy to force the rough, wayward, polyphonous nature of this phenomenon into shapes we already know and then come to foregone conclusions." It is the foregone conclusion that we need to be wary of when writing fiction. It is the foregone conclusion that is hardly ever a part of the actual lived life. It is the foregone conclusion that steals from both reader and writer the experience of intimacy both on and off the page.

I doubt it was my father's intention to marry my mother when he began writing the letters. I am sure marriage was anything but a foregone conclusion when my mother began receiving them. It is easy to take a set of letters like these and overlay them with a fictionalized narrative, one that we recognize in the American myth of romantic love, the belief that there is one perfect person out there for each of us, someone to have and to hold for the rest of our lives. Herein, D'Erasmo warns, lies the grave danger of sentimentality: "The emotions one might wish to have—enduring love, transcendence, lust—which coincidentally are the most socially acceptable emotions in each of their respective situations, are slathered thickly over the story, muffling the emotions that might be more complex, more resistant, more ambiguous."

How to avoid the dangers of sentimentality and the overlay of emotions involves looking not to the characters who are my mother and father but to the space between them. The space between is where we are best able to explore that which is different. Different not only as the Cartesian opposite to the same, dominant, heteronormative tale of happily ever after. This is the different that we best understand through Jacques Derrida's notion of *différance*.

Derrida presents *différance* as a way to challenge what he sees as an artificial separation between speech and writing. In re-creating this word from a space of privilege and power, he begins with the word *différence*, substitutes an *a* for an *e*, and maintains pronunciation even as he completely alters the definition of the term. It's a simple shift in reality offered as a way to explain that *différance* works in temporal and spatial realms, engages with the concept of what it means both to differ and to defer: both to be different and to hold off. In this way, *différance* explores "the movement that structures every dissociation."

Différance, we are told, "is neither a word nor a concept." It cannot be a word because it is the reliability of the word that Derrida seeks to challenge. It cannot be a concept because it does not remain in the intellectual realm, though Derrida would be the first to challenge any phenomenological leanings with which we might want to engage as we deploy *différance*. What is it then?

Derrida assures that *différance* is elusive and knowable; it is a summation, a juncture, an assemblage, a trace, a strategy, a departure. *Différance* is play, it is middle voice, it is necessary, it is unnameable. And yet, even in all of this uncertainty, Derrida assures that, in the end, *différance* is hope. Derrida's presentation of *différance* focuses on the work of language, the instability of meaning in any given word. It engages semiotics, negation, efficacy, historicization. *Différance* enables affect, bodies, multiplicities, somatics. *Différance* can tolerate a move beyond textual linguistic rhetoric and manage material rhetorical manifestation.

The material rhetoric of my father's letters, as texts that evidence continual movement between being in love (with my mother) to being in love (with the love letter) to being in love (with his own art), exhibits *différance* in their material difference.

Each letter simultaneously regresses as it approaches my mother (both the person Patricia O'Brien and the beloved Tricia), ebbs and flows with their shared and differing desires. Collectively, they are an assemblage of *différance*. Most compelling evidence to this effect: when love has been relocated in marriage, the letters cease.

So full of possibility in the beginning, this love he had for his art, the love she had for the artist. To say that it wasn't real, that it was a mistake, that it was doomed from the start would be undercutting everything they created together, everything they would become. To say that it was never meant to be would be naive. Love is at once always and never real.

Here is where these letters begin. With this *différance*. With this *a*: both with his art and with her artist. I find myself here, greeted as the *a* in *différance*. Named at birth as Amy, a girl-child who grows into transgenre writer Ames.

I have spent

a lot of time

thinking about

the word: **o p e n.**

How it is we open letters. How it is we open books. How it is we understand our relationship between letters and books. How language offers us a particular kind of opportunity to open ourselves to each other.

And I think a good place to start is thinking about what it means to be open.

To be open to, with, for, because of, in writing:

in opening writing;

       in opening letters;

       in opening books;

       in o p e n i n g

               o u r

                   s e l v e s.

Con mio amore

Giorgio

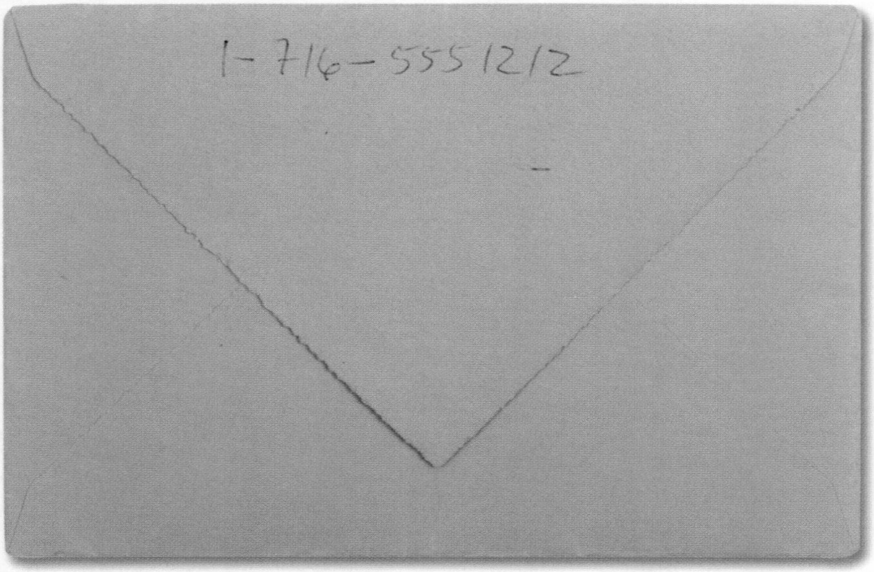
1-716-5551212

1 / August 30, 1966

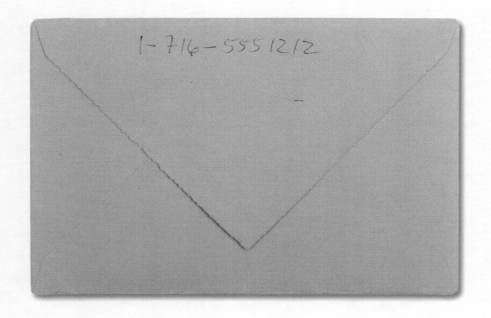

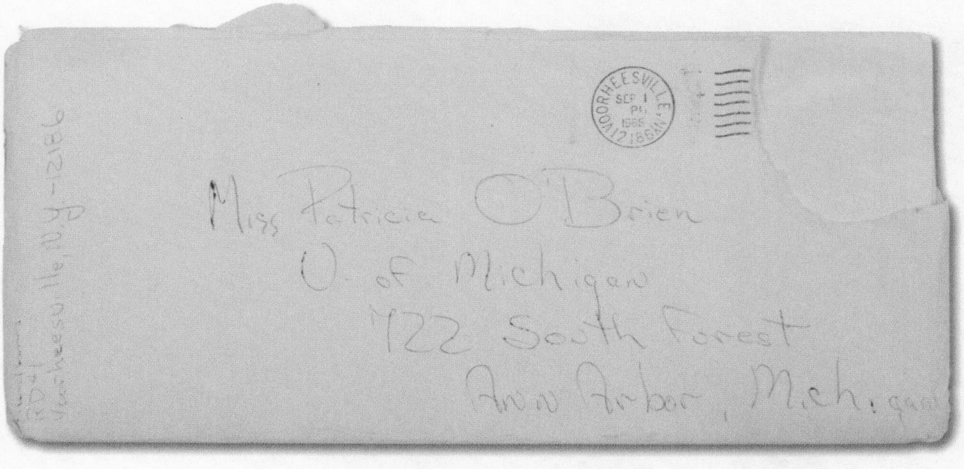

VOORHEESVILLE SEP 1 PM 1966 N.Y. 12186
Miss Patricia O'Brien
U. of Michigan
722 South Forest
Ann Arbor, Mich.

My mother may not know why she kept the letters for so long after they married—so long after they divorced—yet I understand.

Sitting silently inside a cedar chest for over forty years, the letters foretell my parents' fusion, my and my brother's fission; they make sacred that which would otherwise be random.

All so ephemeral without the letters, my existence, the offspring of a gay man once seeking safety and a straight woman desirous of adventure. They serve as a record of an ineffable, whirlwind moment, when a man and a woman moved their relationship from summer fling between boy/kid and girl/coed, to a romantic connection between two lost souls, to a marriage between a man and a woman. A commitment that eventually settles into a life that comes to include me and my brother, two cars, two dogs and a cat, a move from one suburban house to another, a business, a daily life in Grosse Pointe, Michigan.

Letters, as objects—when written, read, and saved— work to mark that which is unmarkable, that which has no mass or matter without their materiality. They evidence a genesis: The beginning of what becomes a simultaneously complex and straightforward life.

With these letters now in my possession, I cannot simply hold onto them but must write about them, respond to the mirrored responses of my mother, the reflective callings of my father. I reply to my own existence in the hope that time, once again, has a chance to breathe. And then, maybe, space has the room to dance.

Hélène Cixous opens her book *Three Steps on the Ladder of Writing*:
"I will begin with:

H

This is what writing is."

She explains that writing is what appears, visually speaking, as a capital I, (one language), set next to another I, (another language), "and between the two the line that makes them vibrate; writing forms a passageway between the two shores." The passageway as translation. The translation as vibration. The vibration as movement between the shores.

H, Cixous tells us, is writing. H is a ladder. H "is the ladder writing climbs, the one that is important to me." A, she explains, same as all the other letters, is masculine. But H, I learn here, "is masculine, neuter, or feminine at will."

I look across and see that I am H. I am me, and I live in two letters, in two lands: A and H. And my writing is the space, the vibration, the translation between the two.

My mother gave to me Derrida's A. My father showed me a "neet path" to Cixous's H. Here, then, I begin. In letters. In these letters: A and H.

And, now, Dear Reader, use your breath. Say it with me as you inflect understanding: **Ah.** Notice where your mind goes as you follow my finger pointing out over the horizon. Recognize me, there: **Ah, yes!** And now your eyes really find focus: **Ah-ha**.

Look hard.

If you do, I am sure that you'll see yourself there, too.

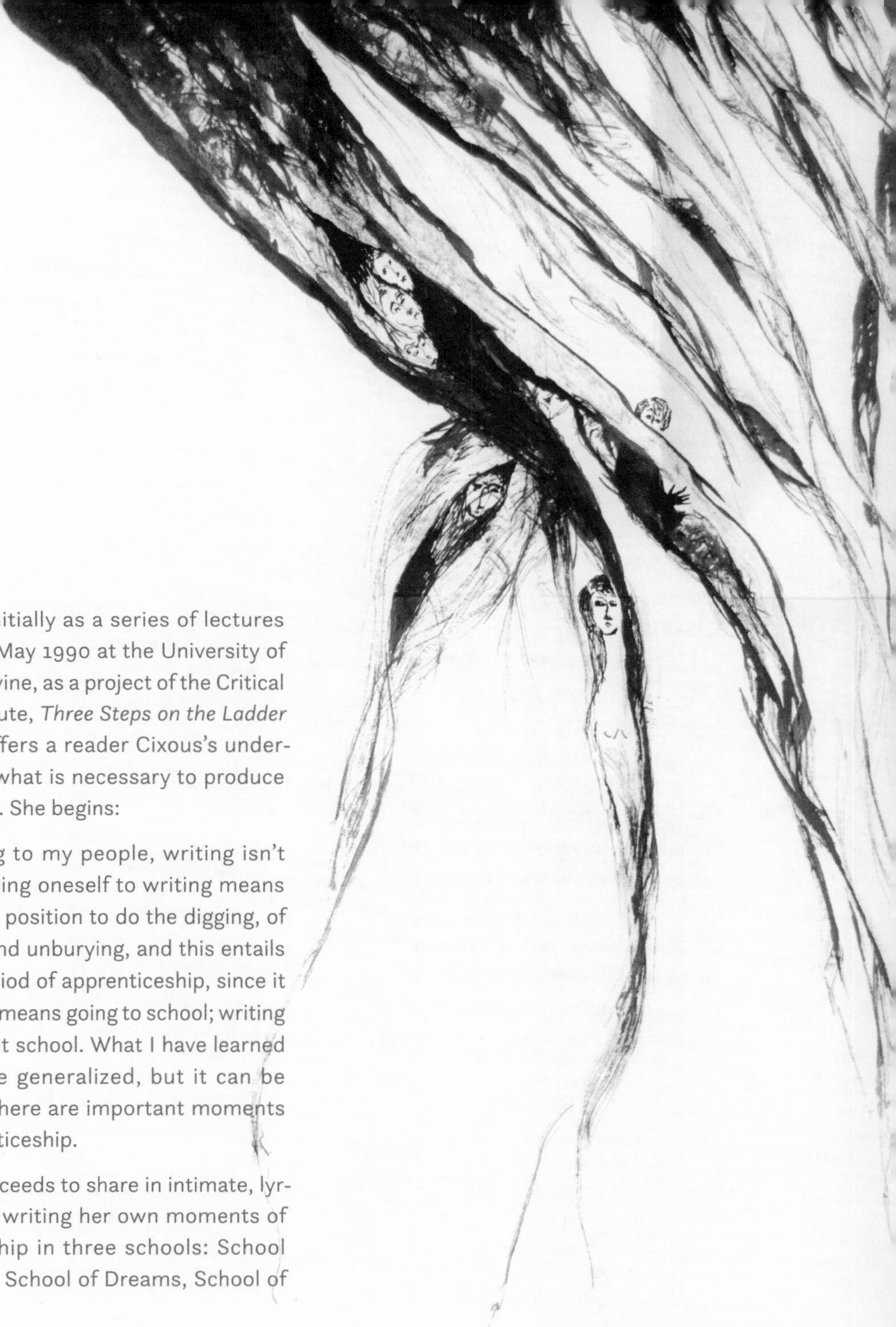

Presented initially as a series of lectures delivered in May 1990 at the University of California, Irvine, as a project of the Critical Theory Institute, *Three Steps on the Ladder of Writing* offers a reader Cixous's understanding of what is necessary to produce great writing. She begins:

> According to my people, writing isn't given. Giving oneself to writing means being in a position to do the digging, of burying and unburying, and this entails a long period of apprenticeship, since it obviously means going to school; writing is the right school. What I have learned cannot be generalized, but it can be shared. There are important moments of apprenticeship.

She then proceeds to share in intimate, lyrical, electric writing her own moments of apprenticeship in three schools: School of the Dead, School of Dreams, School of Roots.

I reflect upon Cixous's ideas regarding apprenticeship, that each school is located in a particular moment, appearing to us, presumably, in order. She offers us the sequence in which we are to dig so as to receive the lessons. But do we apprentice in this order as we live our lives? If so, how could my father, in what is only the second letter, begin with roots? Had he, by the time he was twenty-one, already learned what he needed from the School of the Dead? When did he attend the School of Dreams?

I stare at the image, the one he made as an experiment, something he created by letting his mind wander, and I realize that my father did not begin with roots, at least not in the way that Cixous means. He doesn't enter this idea by using language or composing sentences. He starts by drawing. He creates a visual image that, as he explains, was devised "with no apparent forethought." The young man who writes this piece has no intention of being or becoming and doesn't see himself as a writer. He writes, sure. But, he does not here, nor does he ever, give himself to writing. What the letters tell us, what my mother confers, and what I know to be true is that he sees himself, and wants to see himself, as an artist, a painter.

Yet, Cixous reminds us that writing and painting are not so very far apart. They are connected, in relationship through thinking:

> The thing that is both known and unknown, the most unknown and the best unknown, this is what we are looking for when we write. We go toward the best-known unknown thing, where knowing and not knowing touch, where we hope we will know what is unknown. Where we hope we will not be afraid of understanding the incomprehensible, facing the invisible, hearing the inaudible, thinking the unthinkable, which is of course: thinking. Thinking is trying to think the unthinkable: thinking the thinkable is not worth the effort. Painting is trying to paint what you cannot paint, and writing is writing what you cannot know before you have written: it is preknowing and not knowing blindly with words. It occurs at the point where blindness and light meet.

I am handed the letters in 2009, read them through a first time in 2010, again in 2012, a third time in 2015. During these five years, I say I am writing about these letters. And I do, here and there, in fits and starts, but not in any concentrated, serious way. I say it's because I don't have enough time. I say it's because I'm not quite sure yet what it is I want to say. I say it's because it's ridiculous to write about the love letters of two people who eventually divorce, too self-indulgent to explore how these documents make me who I am.

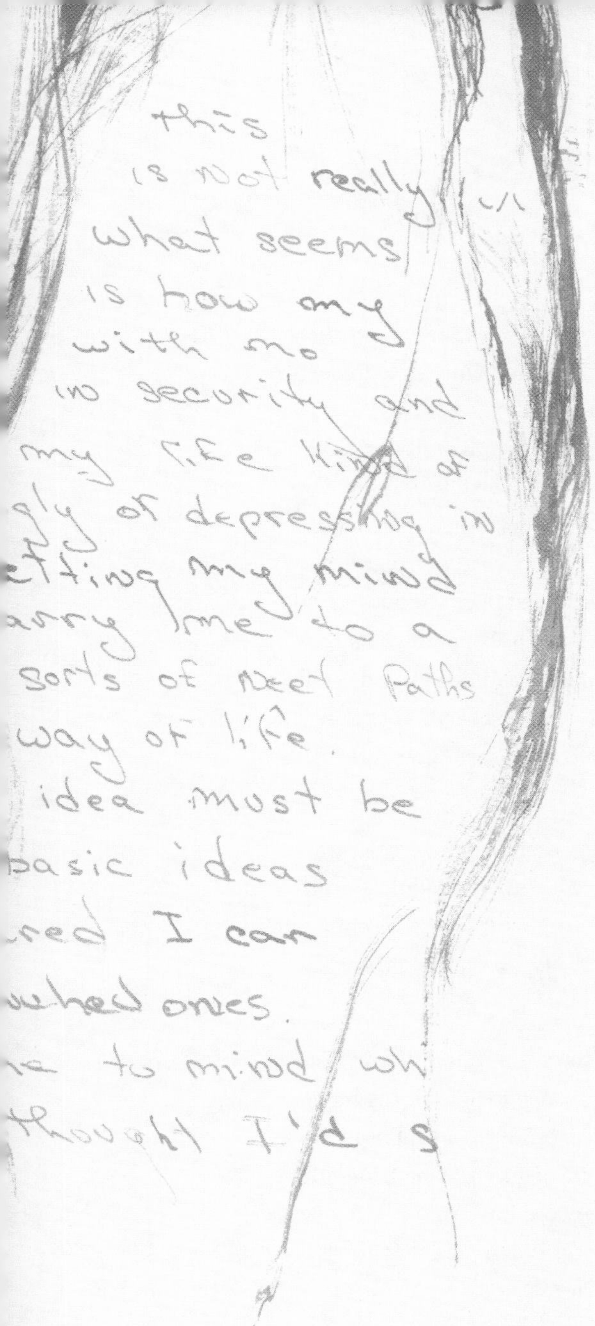

this
is not really c/1
what seems
is how my
with no
no security and
my life kind of
gly of depressing in
etting my mind
aory lme to a
sorts of need paths
way of life.
idea must be
basic ideas
red I can
ached ones.
e to mind wh
thought I'd s

In my darkest moments, I tell myself
I'm not capable.

When I'm feeling merely pessimistic,
I wonder if it's because I don't actually
care.

When I feel a need to self-deprecate,
I decide it's because I have not given
myself to writing.

That I can't and that I probably never will.

Yet, these five years I have been
rediscovering my birthplace.

I have been losing the world.

I have been talking to the dead.

I have, in these ways and places,
been writing.

I have Cixous's words here in my mouth:
"And I said to myself, I wouldn't have written. . . . I wouldn't have had death, if my
father had lived. I have written this several
times: he gave me death. To start with."

I have returned, it seems, so that
I may start.

I have been learning about his art
as my writing.

I have been in school.

I first asked my parents how they met some time when I was about nine or ten. I got a fairly succinct story about them meeting while working at a summer camp for special needs children in upstate New York while they were still in college. My mother had come from the University of Michigan to fulfill a requirement for her teaching degree. She was employed as a tutor. My father, a student at Buffalo State College, was returning for his second summer as a camp counselor. The first year the placement was recommended by his school program. He landed at camp the second time because he had just returned from a semester in Siena, Italy, had not yet secured summer employment, didn't want to live at home, and really didn't know what else to do. Then they got married, got an apartment, had me, bought a house, had my brother, moved one more time to Grosse Pointe, and that, it seemed, was that.

I never really questioned any of it then, but other evidence regarding timing didn't quite make sense. They celebrated their wedding anniversary on September 25, but in their wedding pictures my mother is wearing a sleeveless yellow dress and the time stamp on the slim white border says Apr '67.

I asked for the story a couple more times over the years, but it wasn't until my mother gave me the letters—not until I was able to hold in my hands the evidence that there had been intense passion, a once-upon-a-time electric connection—that I not only wanted but somehow became able to know more about their initial meeting; when and how they fell in love. In 2007, sixteen years following their divorce, an independent inquiry of each of my parents revealed a strikingly similar tale.

At first, neither was interested in the other. My mother had a "work-based" relationship with my father since she tutored many of his campers, and, during the first four-week session, she would often talk with him in the evenings about how the campers were doing, how he and she might work together to best serve the children. In between sessions all camp employees were granted a thirty-six-hour leave. My dad told it this way: "Everyone else had made plans. Before we knew it, your mother and I were the last ones there, just staring at each other. I looked at her and said, 'Do you want to go swim in the ocean?' She said she did, and we drove to Connecticut to do just that." They corroborated: Following a day at the ocean, they drove back to his parents' house, spent the night, and drove back to camp. Once back at camp, they were officially an item. Four weeks later, she returned to Ann Arbor and he started writing her letters—for about a month, until they were married, until they made plans for her to move to Buffalo at the end of October.

When I asked my father, knowing what he knew then—that he was gay, that he had purposefully (as he used to tell it) entered homosexual deprogramming two years prior to meeting my mother, that there really wasn't the kind of passion there that we assume underpins romantic love—why it was he and my mother married, he was as clear as he was reflective: "We were two lost souls who found each other." When I told my mother what he said, she steadily and succinctly agreed: "That about sums it up."

In these letters, my father constantly and continually declares his love for my mother. Yet, these letters also reveal another beloved: his own thinking and art. I am nowhere in these letters, and yet I am on every single page. These letters as Then and me as Now. This moment a bridge between the two. These letters are my roots; they are the trunk of our family tree. These letters—love of letters—are where I, as writer (my writing), begin.

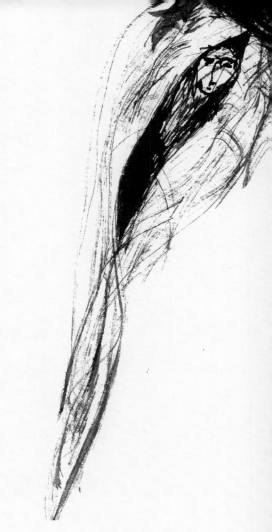

These [LETTERS] (are-inhale) ((our-exhale)) places.

This [BOOK] (my-inhale) ((as-exhale)) work.

2 / September 1, 1966

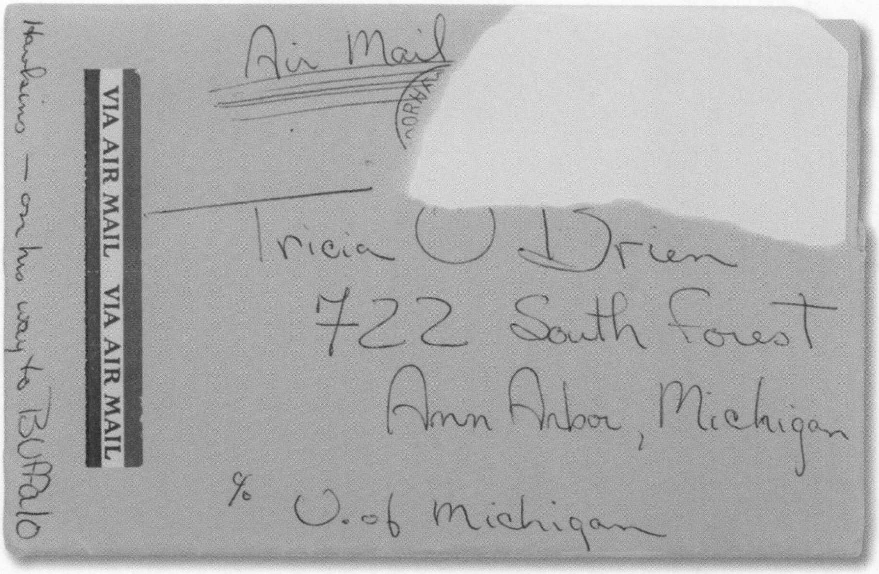
Air Mail
VIA AIR MAIL VIA AIR MAIL
— on his way to BUFFALO
Tricia O'Brien
722 South Forest
Ann Arbor, Michigan
c/o U. of Michigan

Rather than using envelopes, Emily Dickinson preferred
to fold her letters to Susan Huntington Gilbert Dickinson,
sometimes in quarters, sometimes in thirds.

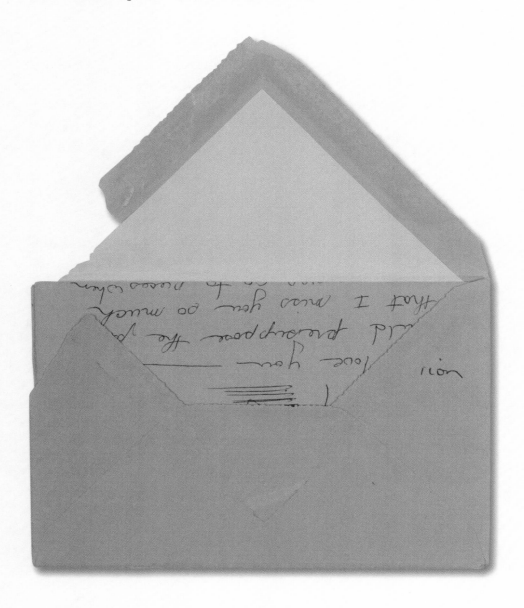

Many exhibit pinholes, the tiniest of openings, traces of Emily's material relationship with these missives. She'd often pin them inside the pocket of her apron or dress, waiting until they could be delivered. Sometimes she'd hand the letter to a child in the family, or someone working in the home, and have them deliver the letter to Susan. Emily and Susan, sisters-in-law, lived next door to one another.

I sit and think about the one sweet directive written in the fold of a letter from June 1852: "Open me, carefully." A delicate bidding; tender instruction, clarified by the sentiment that Susan do so at once, full of care. I imagine Susan detecting the energetic shadow of Emily's touch, tracing folds with fingers, hand with eye, and in this mirroring moment I find myself in compositional communion with Emily imagining her trust.

Here: Here are my words. Please be gentle with them. I am made vulnerable here for you on the page. Open, please, open. But know that when you do, I will be splayed wide exposed for your consideration, as a rupture of words and ideas and language now contained, soon to be dangerously unfurled.

I understand Anaïs Nin writing to Henry Miller: "I have become an idiot like Gertrude Stein. That's what love does to intelligent women. They cannot write letters anymore."

I hold tight Hélène Cixous's confession that she likes the first sentence of *O Lustro*, by Clarice Lispector. She likes "a book that begins like this. It begins inside, in the body. These are books you can read. These are real books. You open the book and you have already crossed the border."

Phone call from my father, spring 2006.

A: Dad, I just wanted to let you know that I'm going write about you and my relationship with you on the *Critical Encounters* blog this year.

G: Oh, OK.

A: So, I'm telling you because it's the ethical thing to do. I'm going to out you, Dad, in all ways.

G: Like I give a shit.

A: I know, but I needed to tell you. Maybe you can write something for the blog sometime.

G: Listen, I may not be able to go with you on Sunday to your brother's house because I have to go to the dentist. My teeth are falling out.

A: I thought they had been falling out.

G: Well, I had been being careful and watching what I ate. They hadn't fallen out yet, but I coughed at work yesterday and a tooth came out in my hand. They are all dead.

A: That really sucks.

G: Yeah, it does. I had to get over that, I had to pull myself together, and then get myself down to Walgreens to get something so I could glue it back in.

A: You glued it back in?

G: Yeah.

A: So, what are you going to do?

G: I'm going to call 1-800-DENTIST and see who will deal with me.

A: Do you have any time left at work? Vacation?

G: I have ten days. But I don't want to use it for this.

A: Maybe you want to think about retiring early and take the ten days to get your ducks in a row.

G: Yeah, I have to do that.

A: Let me know and I can come with you to get a case worker. We just need a heads-up.

G: Yeah, I have to do that.

pause

G: I put myself back on Ensure, but I haven't really been able to eat for quite a while.

A: Dad, you can't live on Ensure!

G: It has done the trick pretty well, but I still lose weight. So, it'll be good to eat again.

A: Dad, Ensure will not sustain you for the duration.

pause

A: Well, just tell us and we can come and help you.

G: Yeah, OK, well, I wasn't even going to call until I had an appointment.

A: So, call and tell us when the appointment is and what you need.

G: OK, I guess I'll be spending the next few months at the dentist and at doctors. What else do I have to do?

A: It's what there is to do. This is what to do.

G: Yeah, I'll call you later.

A: OK, talk with you soon, Dad.

G: OK, bye.

love

My jaw dropped when I realized that more than forty years before my father hacked a tooth into his hand, he wrote about an anxiety about losing his teeth. Why did my father open a letter to my mother in this way? Did he think it was funny? Intimate? Strange? We might guess that he was afraid. Of going to Vietnam. Of dying in Vietnam. Of dying, it appears, without any of his teeth.

> The Dentist was fun — we talked about teeth (logically) and the fact mine are still in my mouth and with all seeming intent to stay there — unless I contact some rare tropical disease in Viet Nam. Would you still love me if all my teeth fell out and I had to gum my food to death?

In the first year after he moved from Detroit to Chicago, when he'd come over for dinner, we'd watch him flinch and grimace as he'd chew. It was unnerving, disturbing. Painful to watch, worse to ignore.

Once, I asked him, "Dad, what's up with your chewing? Something is wrong with your teeth." "I just bit my cheek," he said. I knew that he'd never admit that his teeth were falling out.

Not until he had to, when they actually did.

When my father told me about losing a tooth at work, I pictured the dream sequence in *The Sopranos* when Tony spits a bloody tooth into his

The letter is a magical genre that has the potential to show you—as writer/reader—your self as

hand. I found myself repulsed and excited by the imagery. Most people aren't subject to the disgrace invoked by sudden, unpredicted, non-pugilistic tooth loss. One might argue that it wasn't unpredictable—his teeth had been falling out for years. But the predictability of projectile dentition remains elusive. It really isn't something to imagine or anticipate. It was evidence of the absurd.

What caused his teeth to rot and fall out? If you ask me, I'll tell you he had necrotic ulcerative periodontitis. Put as simply as possible, damage caused by the HIV virus was causing his gums to rot and his teeth to fall out. More of a condition than a disease, NUP is caused by the conversion from HIV to AIDS, which accelerates the degeneration of oral health. That and the long-term use of antiviral drugs place an immense amount of stress on the mouth.

love

I never knew this to be a condition of AIDS. All the pictures I saw of young men in the 1980s wasting in beds had these huge, grotesque, white teeth. In those days, AIDS patients were getting sick and dying so fast their gums never had the chance to rot, their teeth the opportunity to loosen, let alone fall out. With advances in health care and a relative arsenal of pharmaceuticals, people are living (longer) with HIV. Antiretroviral drugs and prophylactic medications have caused a shift in the bodily impact of the HIV virus. Death due to rare infections such as Kaposi sarcoma, pneumocystis pneumonia, and multifocal leukoencephalopathy (a demyelinating disease of the central nervous system) has dropped off considerably in the past thirty years. In the transition of the HIV infection from acute to chronic, HIV- and AIDS-related deaths are most often ascribed to the culturally normative groupings of cardiovascular disease (stroke and heart attack), non-AIDS-related cancers, and suicide.

When I asked my dad why he was losing his teeth, he told me that he had begun losing his molars shortly following his heart attack a few years back, and he was sure there was a connection. When my mother asked, my father told her that he was losing his teeth because of all the orthodontia he had had in the 1980s.

love. How did I learn to write letters? When did I grow to love them? How, I wonder, did I ever

My mother and I asked my father about his teeth, I believe, because we wanted some "information." We wanted something about this mysterious illness to be knowable. If we could know why his teeth were falling out, we could allay our guilt, resolve our fears, and organize the chaos of our shared experience of George's disintegration.

But my dad never played by the rules of the HIV and AIDS story. He was never going to provide us with facts, truth, or any of the particular details that would allow us to use, present, and/or represent his narrative in a unified way. While it may have been frustrating for me and my mother at the time, I now see that as his absolute right. His death, his life, his story. OK.

When my father's teeth fell out, in that moment of crisis, he sought dental care. He found a dentist who turned his four bottom teeth into a temporary bridge. According to my father, the dentist also performed a deep cleaning and prescribed the removal of all of his teeth and the creation of dentures. According to my father, this would be extremely expensive, and he "just didn't have the money." According to my father, he couldn't get the dentures right then because he didn't have the time off from work to be toothless for weeks while his mouth healed.

love

A year before he died, my father's teeth were removed, and he acquired a set of dentures. I never knew for sure, but I imagine that the doctors made him take care of the situation, made the appointments for him. He had since retired and was on Medicaid. He would, at this point, neither have to take time off from work nor have to pay for the procedure himself.

He also had no choice.

He had, as was his way, left the situation to the situation, which always, in the end, took care of itself.

Her attraction began as a kind of disgust, disrespect borne on a repeated pattern of his never having enough money, of always being the person to order nothing more than a glass of water at a restaurant and then accept the food offered by others around the table, of consistently being the only one in the circle to bum cigarettes and never have any to offer. The other counselors and camp staff seemed not to notice, but this behavior so challenged her own personal sense of dignity that she began secretly watching and waiting for him to mooch off the group. She didn't talk about him with the other counselors. She kept to herself. But she stared at his hands, wondering whether they would ever reach into pants pockets, ever bring forth any resource whatsoever.

Maybe it was because he felt her judgment, a raw self-righteous assessment, that he worked on cultivating a visceral dislike for her. Who did she think she was to judge him and the other kids so harshly? Each night she, under the pretext of being the camp tutor, came to his cabin to talk about child development and individual student progress. He smirked and smoked her cigarettes as she ably converted his campers into her students. He wasn't going to correct her. The thing was he didn't actually care, having taken this job for the second summer in a row simply to avoid living under the same roof as his father. He didn't give a shit that she was so uptight, that she came to his cabin every night to tell him what he might do to support her in tutoring the children, that she had a habit of clearing her throat right before saying the name of someone she didn't like. It had an appeal, actually, this self-possessed snobby confidence. Seemed to underscore the natural beauty of her eyebrows, the broad perfection of her smile.

Perhaps because he believed he was in alignment with the other counselors, he was more surprised than she to find himself staring at her, the two of them left without particular invitations, without specific plans for their thirty-six-hour break between camp sessions. She hadn't sought any invitation from the others, didn't like the idea of getting sloppy drunk and screwing in the sand. So, maybe she felt relieved when she was left, after all the others had already gone, staring at him. Perhaps it was because she had no more idea than he did of how to spend the next day and a half that she graciously, even before he asked, before she took a cigarette from the pack herself, offered one to him. He smiled, removed two smokes, simultaneously lit them, and handed one to her. They stood in the middle of the dirt road that connected the staff parking lot to the main camp, staring across the field where the campers played evening games of capture the flag and freezer tag, silently drawing on the filters of two of her Winstons.

With the final exhale, before dropping the smoldering butt to the ground, he tossed off a proposal that would have sounded to an outsider as though he knew what she was thinking, as though they had known each other for years: *Want to go to the ocean?*

Her answer was equally familiar: *Sure.*

Most of the car ride was silent save for the tympanic wind whipping through the open windows.

It was her car; she drove. Occasionally, he or she would draw a cigarette from a pack—hers of course—on the seat in the space between them. He spent most of the time staring out the window, head cocked slightly toward his left shoulder. She spent most of the time watching the road, occasionally looking over at him, eyes fixed on the space between his left earlobe and the collar of his shirt. What surprised them both was their level of ease: with themselves, with each other. Lack of care to impress had settled into gentle comfort. Two hours after getting in the car in upstate New York, they stood on a beach in Connecticut, wading in the Atlantic.

Once on the sand, they chatted in bits and pieces. He knew a few of the people from the year before, so he had stories to tell, and they found an initial common ground in their dislike for certain other staff members. Her laugh, her smile, made him feel buoyant—light—and he began feigning disgust with the seagulls, squealing and sprinting away from them, only to pivot and run screaming into an entire flock that had come to land on the beach, hopeful that a vacationer might decide to toss them some chips, or crackers, or the crusts from wax paper–wrapped sandwiches.

Though she didn't join him in his youthful play, she smiled and delighted in his joy, laughed out loud when he began singing in a faux opera falsetto, moving from addressing them as an entire audience to singling out one lone bird that hadn't yet flown away in fear. Her laughter entered his chest, erupting into explosions of what might only be understood as his own self-acceptance. He heard her and somehow felt more able to listen to himself. And so, he wanted to talk.

He regaled her with stories as they walked along the water's edge. Stared into the sand as he told her about having lived in New York City, as well as in Siena, Italy, that previous winter semester. About having once met Allen Ginsberg, about being sure he had once recognized Picasso on the street. He spoke highly of his mother, respectfully of his father, and lovingly of his crazy aunt. It was Aunt G who had nurtured his artistic soul, invited him to her room, where he might, on any given afternoon throughout his boyhood and teenage years, watch her paint, or feed and talk with her birds, or arrange flowers, or tat lace. When Aunt G's eyes became bad, she asked him to read her poetry: Wordsworth, Longfellow, cummings, and all the other noteworthy Yankees. Aunt G confirmed what he knew in his heart, that what he wanted, more than anything, was to be an artist.

As he spoke, she watched his feet imprints in the sand, watched them fall into step with her own. She had never met anyone like him. Never anyone who had been so many places, done so many things. He was so odd, so interesting. So different. She kept silent, preferring these tales of excitement to the daily narrative created by the lackluster reality of a dying mother and a workaholic father. He talked, and they walked until they ran out of beach, the tide having removed their ability to make it around a giant pile of boulders at the end of an arc of land. It was late afternoon, but summer, so there was plenty of light left in the day.

Meeting her gaze and smiling easily, he tossed off another spontaneous, casual question: *You want to go meet my parents?*

It wasn't only because they couldn't yet return to camp that she said, *Yes.*

Any child might identify in their parents' love letters a corporeal commencement, might be able to say: without these letters I would not exist. But for me, there is extra weight, awareness redoubled in realizing that what my father has lettered here, has let onto the page, is not only my genesis as a flesh-and-blood person, but the inception of my place in and with relationship to lineage and legacy, to writing itself. What my mind knows and my body now feels: My parents were both adopted. From their hands to mine, the body of the letters as mine, I think, these are love letters. In this moment, I place my fingers on the reiterated pulse of their attraction, re-pulsing this thought:

The Midwest—Michigan—is where I am from. These letters, though?

Here is where I am born.

love

49

elp cut down on
the Number of
cigarettes in circulation
Smoke more!

3 / September 6, 1966

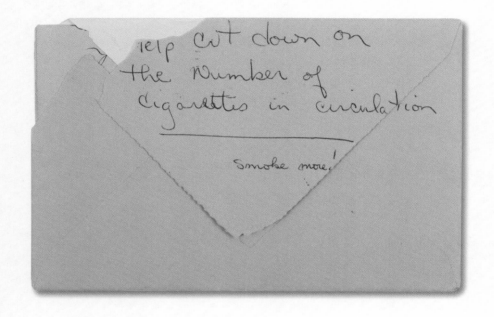

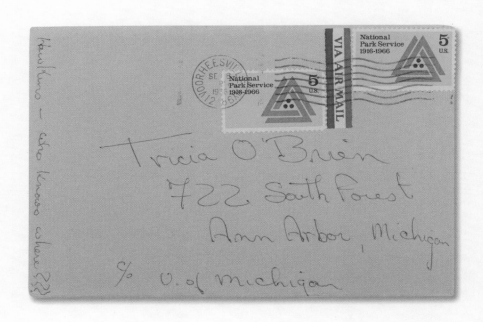

Tricia O'Brien
722 South Forest
Ann Arbor, Michigan

c/o U. of Michigan

VIA AIR MAIL

National Park Service 1916-1966 5 U.S.

National Park Service 1916-1966 5 U.S.

VOORHEESVILLE

My sixteen-year-old son notices *The 50 Greatest Love Letters of All Time*, edited by David H. Lowenherz, on the top of a stack of published love letter collections: "These are the fifty greatest. The greatest. The *Greatest*," he says.

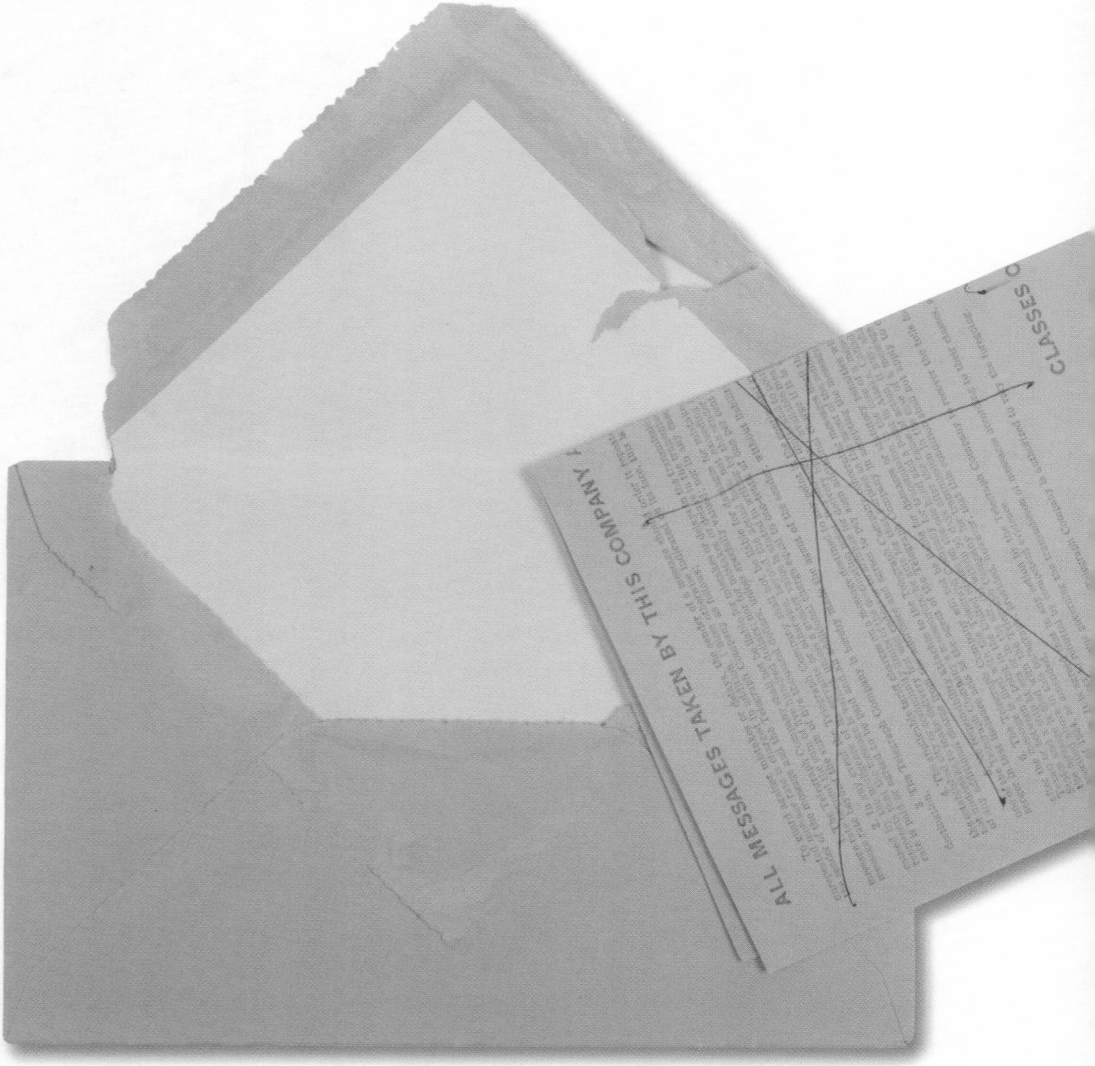
ALL MESSAGES TAKEN BY THIS COMPANY
CLASSES

TELEGRAM
DAY LETTER (DL)
NIGHT LETTER (NL)

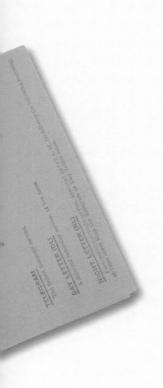

He turns his face to mine, widens his eyes with subtle sarcasm, pauses for effect. My smile makes clear I appreciate his humor, so he continues. "This," another purposeful pause, "this is it." He sweeps an open-palmed hand majestically in front of the stack. "All. Just: Done. We don't need to write any more. And, nope. None of these other ones," he deadpans, his hand now vertically undulating in front of the pile, "do we even—ever—need to read."

I laugh out loud. Partly because I know he's a little bit making fun of me and my stacks (and stacks) of books and partly because I haven't read hardly any of the letters reprinted in the volumes piled here. No more than two of the supposed "fifty greatest" and only a few of the *Love Letters from Famous People*, edited by Estela Raileanu. There have to be people out there who've read all, or even most, of *Love Letters: 2,000 Years of Romance*, edited by Andrea Clarke, or Ursula Doyle's *The Love Letters of Great Men*, or the more inclusive *Love Letters of Great Men and Women*, edited by C. H. Charles, but, admittedly, their readerships do not include me. I did thumb through *The Virago Book of Love Letters*, edited by Jill Dawson, but spent more time thinking about the table of contents and her identification of there being different categories, such as Invitation, Declaration, and Adulation, than I did reading.

Whether or not anyone else has been interested enough to actually read these collections of letters is impossible to know, though I imagine there are some who would spend the time with them. Reading these documents offers a way of gaining context for a particular moment. I am sure there are those interested in a more intimate look at the

lives of particular artists and politicians. There's also the possibility that the power of reading the love letters of famous, historically relevant people brings us into communion with their power, a connection via the common human experience of love.

Yet, whether or not the letters get read seems less relevant to me than the work of publishing them, making them available, adding them to and bringing them into relationship with all of the other love letter collections. We can't know whether folks actually read these collections, but we do know that there has been a definite increase in the publication of these sorts of volumes during the last twenty years. It could be that the letters themselves have been recently released into the public domain, that they're being published now because access to them is new. It could be because we have a different, emergent interest in archives and archival materials. It could be that we're now experiencing some kind of premature nostalgia for the loss of the love letter itself, a communicative form we assume is dying—perhaps even nearly dead—because of the ways email and texting have made the hard copy letter seem obsolete. Regardless, publishing these letter collections creates a critical mass of work that calls attention to the power and purpose of the love letter as a rhetorical genre.

Written with the intention and hope for clarity, personal letters don't carry the burden of concision, efficiency, or linear logic. The goal is to reinforce or restructure a relationship; to offer an apology, condolences, thanks; to declare to a particular person, "I love you," whether using these particular three words in this precise order or not.

Bodies of letters describe and inscribe our most intimate connections. Not only those we have with each other, but the ones that we have, seek, and desire with ourselves.

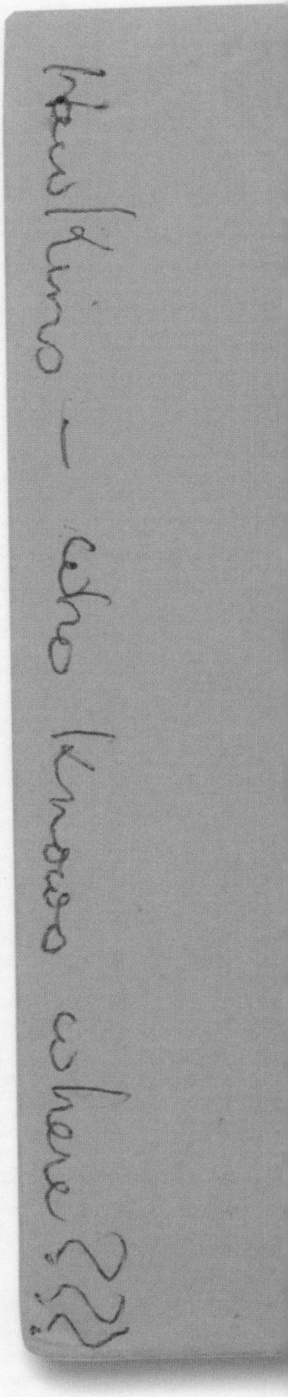

My first year of high school, I and all of my peers at Grosse Pointe South were provided a copy of *Basic English Revisited: A Student Handbook*. In the days before the Internet, this thin, 125-page, bright yellow, hardcover book offered quick and easy access to a wide range of information including writing mechanics, basic grammar rules, a table of weights and measures, the American Sign Language alphabet, and my personal favorite, the signs of the zodiac.

For years, I turned again and again to the section on The Letter. In my copy, there on pages 61 and 62, you'll find a large hand-drawn asterisk in pencil and a blue-inked five-pointed star, my visual cues to easily locate information such as: Which comes first, my address or the one to whom I was writing? How many spaces are there between the date and my greeting? Where do I place my closing? How might I sign my name?

All through high school and college, on the same shelf, not far from *Basic English Revisited*, sat another important reference book: *The Official Preppy Handbook*. Published in 1980, this satirical volume by Lisa Birnbach felt as true and relevant to me as *Basic English*, offering equally important information to assist me with negotiating my existence as a stellar student-athlete-good-"girl" who felt alternately accepted and rejected for how I looked, behaved, moved, achieved.

Chided with phrases such as "Easy there, Slugger" and "Calm down, Butch," I was often taunted by boys, and sometimes teased by girls, as much for how I walked as for making particularly successful plays in gym. But I was also aware that Title IX and Birnbach's explanation of the "Basic Body Types" made being female, intellectual, and good at sports possible in my preppy, Anglophilic, WASPy hometown.

love

In 1980s America, being preppy was popular; in Grosse Pointe it was *authentic*. Preppy was what the town had always been and, at that time, seemed as though it would always be. Though located squarely in the Midwest, much of the aesthetic and sensibilities felt particularly East Coast, aesthetically and aspirationally connected with places like the Hamptons and Martha's Vineyard; with Izod, Jack Rogers, and Madewell; with yellow and blue seersucker; with Nantucket red; with paisley: pink and green.

It wasn't just that I was there, visible in the pages of *The Official Preppy Handbook*, as some sort of cross between two of the female types—the Amazon and the Party Girl. In one small, unassuming passage, Birnbach's book made space for those of us who move beyond particular gender roles, identifying the possibility for existing somewhere in between:

> When the male and female traits seem to have switched genders, you have the Aesthete and the Amazon. The Aesthete often looks as if his voice hasn't changed but will any minute. Everything a man—or the Aesthete—could want the Amazon has; mostly a torso that could make Steve Reeves jealous.

I had no idea who Steve Reeves was, but it didn't matter. In these pages, I learned about the mythical possibility of becoming *both* the Aesthete *and* the Amazon. By the magical transference made possible through this short description, despite both the names I was called as a child and the fact that I felt it necessary at sixteen to adopt femme drag in order to better fit in, Grosse Pointe presented me the possibility of a future when I would feel completely comfortable as myself, in my own skin. On the shelf, flanked by *Basic English* and *The Official Preppy Handbook*, I located the promise of my future *in between*.

Had a friend of mine not mentioned it, I doubt I'd have ever found *Darlinghissima: Letters to a Friend*, by Janet Flanner, a volume edited by Natalia Danesi Murray, the woman with whom Flanner had a thirty-eight-year "passionate friendship." The letters offer an extraordinary account of politics, art, writing, and love as recorded by one of the many Paris-relocated twentieth-century expatriate writers, Janet Flanner, the badass foreign correspondent for the *New Yorker*, who wrote as Genêt in "Letters from Paris" on a biweekly basis from 1925 to 1975, interrupted only by World War II. Flanner was a woman of uncommon grace and intellectual acumen, a lady who verbally sparred with Ernest Hemingway, knew and hung out with the likes of Gertrude Stein, Alice B. Toklas, Mary McCarthy, Carson McCullers, Elsa Schiaparelli, Walter Lippman, and Colette, and got invited to Truman Capote's and the Rothschilds' balls.

love

Flanner tells of her reaction to the March on Washington, the death of John F. Kennedy, the escalation and end of the Vietnam War. Descriptions of weather and flowers, where she ate, her love of and appreciation for stylish clothing, her writing process, her self-doubt, her health, and plans for her next connection with Murray make these missives rich, complicated, human reads. Murray, in her narration and editing of the letters, becomes as present and relevant as Flanner, offering the reader narrative bridges between correspondences, cultural

context, and personal insights when necessary. What we have been given by Murray, in the reprinting of these letters, is a wealth of information and perspective just waiting to be mined.

Yet, what I find most compelling about the letters are the greetings, the openings. More specifically, I am taken with the terms of endearment Flanner chooses for her love. Over the course of the thirty-year correspondence, we learn that Murray was her "Darling," "My darling one," "Sweetheart," "Darlingest," "Dearling," "Carissima," "Precious." She was her "blessed Natalia," "my Beloved," "Darling Creature," "Darling Beloved." She was her "Sweetest Heart," "Darling Natalia," "Natalia cara," "Dearest Voice," "Beloved," and, once, "Mon petit coq en pate." Natalia was her "Darlingest one," "My poor darling," "Beloved sprite," "Mon amour," "My precious." She was her "Beloved traveler," "Dear One," and, once, "My love."

Darlinghissima, the choice of title for the book, becomes the most oft-repeated opening other than variations of "Darling," the English version of this Italian word, and presents November 11, 1950, as the first date Flanner greets Murray as such. Thirty-nine *darlinghissimas* follow, including a few one-time variations: "My darlinghissima, my blessed Natalia, Buon Natale," "Friday, my darlinghissima, carissima," "Darlinghissima mia," "Bellissima, tenderissima, darlinghissima," and, once, my favorite in the collection, "Darlinghissimassima."

Darlinghissima
Darling
My darling one
Sweetheart
Darlingest
Dearling
Carissima
Precious
blessed Natalia
my Beloved
Darling Creature
Darling Beloved
Sweetest Heart
Darling Natalia
Natalia cara
Dearest Voice
Beloved
Mon petit coq en pâte
Darlingest one
My poor darling
Beloved sprite
Mon amour
My precious
Beloved traveler
Dear One
My love

Through these greetings, Janet opens for and to and with Natalia. She opens over and over and over again, and in reprinting these openings here, Murray opens for us as well. They, in this epistolary relationship, open and reopen the space of possibility for love as it exists without a cultural label, without a marker for anyone except each other. It is this opening, this vulnerability, this unfettered accessibility that strikes me so; makes me honored and privileged, sure of the gift these women have given the world through these words.

How these letters open for me, how they help me think about the work of openings, invitations, beginnings, and my own access to risk. How the greeting has the power to break into the reader's day, offering a certain rupture into the usual sense of time and space, preoccupies my thought.

As both declaration of and for desire, the opening reveals the writer's state of mind, allows us the false sense that we understand what they mean—meant—to each other. Our understanding, I realize, by the time the letter closes, coming only from wondering whether and how and to whom I've ever opened like this, what it meant when I did, what it means when any of us becomes uniquely available to another on the page, using words and terms of endearment all our own.

These letters were given to me, but they are never only mine. They are my father's writing, his art.

So, what is that purpose, the point of the love letter? Obvious, you might say: The purpose of the love letter is to declare love. The love letter provides both an outlet for the felt need to say, "I love you," and a way to convince and/or ascertain whether the beloved loves the writer, too.

The love letter provides a way to bridge a gap in space and time, to connect oneself, as my father did, with and to another, despite physical distance. In many of the letters, my father writes about what it feels like to use the letters as a way to "talk" with my mother. He wrote to her all hours of the day and night. Whenever, it seems, he wanted to feel as though he were there virtually, if not physically, sitting next to her in the same room. He desired what he described as being together with her in "their world." There's no doubt in my mind that he was holding onto their summertime love affair by writing to her, that he returned to the sensations he felt in those moments with her by writing to her. And since the letters end soon after they marry, weeks before my mother moves to Buffalo, it's also clear that it was physical proximity he wanted most of all. Evidence that also supports the assumption that the genre has waned because email and texting collapse this distance more quickly, more profoundly—ergo, better—than a pen, paper, and stamp ever could.

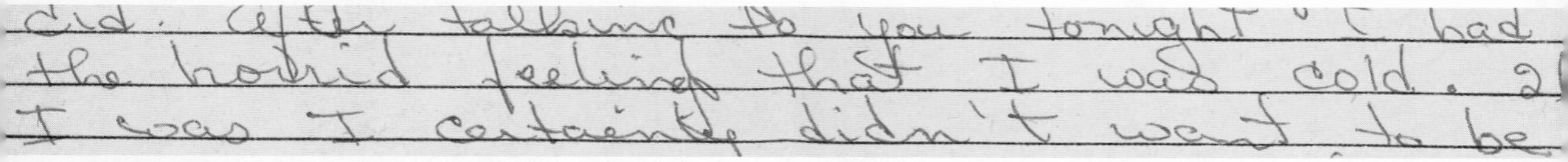
did. After talking to you tonight I had
the horrid feeling that I was cold. If
I was I certainly didn't want to be

Gifts he once gave to her, family history then handed down to me. My remaking of them a legacy.

The basic form of the letter hasn't changed much at all in the two thousand years of recognized history of the genre. Letters by Cicero, Seneca, and Petrarch, as well as the oldest original surviving letters we've got, those discovered in 1973 at a Roman outpost in Northern Britain called Vindolanda, are generally composed of three main parts: (1) heading/greeting/opening, (2) body, (3) closing/signature.

But learning about the form of a letter doesn't necessarily tell us much about the work of the form; how to work it, what and how to write. Predictably, shortly following recognition of the form, there was the production of how-to advice. Some of the first direction regarding how to write a letter, positioned as categorization regarding different rhetorical purposes. The basic public-private distinction is credited to a little-known Aristotle-quoting scholar named Libanius/Demetrius, whose tract scholars have narrowed down to having been written sometime in the eight hundred years occurring between the fourth centuries BC and AD.

One could almost choose any historical era and identify some sort of how-to guide regarding the proper and/or effective writing of letters. The explosion of letter writing following governmental regulation of mail in the mid-1800s in the United States and Britain presented a host of how-to books aimed at those who may have been new to the form, wanting to get in on what was a kind of communicative rage. Victorianism inspired its own etiquette-focused letter-writing advice, which was carried over into the twentieth century in the popular publications of Emily Post. Judith Martin took over concerns and laments the loss of the form, yet updates her advice for the twenty-first century and provides commentary regarding when and how to employ proper use of email. A handwritten, postmarked letter remains the preferred epistle of choice.

love

This book is a project in connecting to the divine as design.

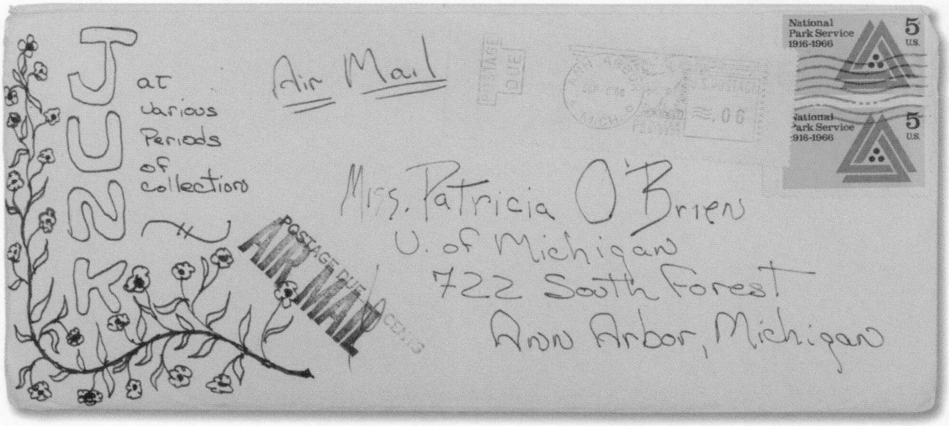
JUNK
at various Periods of collection
Air Mail
POSTAGE DUE
National Park Service 1916-1966 5 U.S.
National Park Service 1916-1966 5 U.S.
Miss. Patricia O'Brien
U. of Michigan
722 South Forest
Ann Arbor, Michigan
AIR MAIL
POSTAGE DUE CENTS

AIR MAIL
POSTAGE DUE

AIR MAIL
POSTAGE DUE

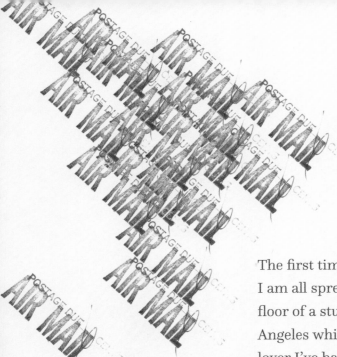

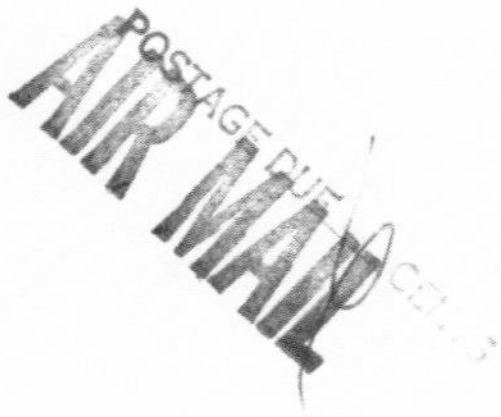

The first time I read the letters,
I am all spread out on a wood
floor of a studio apartment in Los
Angeles while, feet away, the first
lover I've had in fifteen years sleeps.
Here, removed by more than two
thousand miles from my mother,
brother, life partner and children,
I can finally read the letters because
here, in this space suspended
outside and beyond my life, in a
space between, I can breathe.

Here, in this moment, with these
objects, I am in and of; because of
and with; here, in this moment,
I: am.

I began writing about my father believing I was working on a "new" AIDS memoir, one that didn't focus on untimely death, wasn't written from the perspective of the lover or best friend. I wanted to use my father's life and experience to explore what it meant to live with AIDS rather than die from it. What it meant to be the child of someone with HIV&AIDS, someone who contracted the disease after we knew of its existence and how it could be medically treated.

I read hundreds of books about the subject, learned about the government's refusal to acknowledge the disease. I became enthralled by the stories of activist groups such as ACT UP and its art activist sister Gran Fury and the ways they put pressure on the government to acknowledge and then provide monetary support for research, effect change in the Food and Drug Administration's guidelines regarding experimental drugs so that people had access to interventions as soon as possible. I learned about the ways that early identification of the "4H's"—homosexuals, heroin addicts, hemophiliacs, and Haitians—as risk groups created for the virus rhetorical connection with and to familiar cultural frames of discrimination and racism. I wondered about the same impact our factual teachings today regarding the ways HIV transmission occurs—through blood, semen, vaginal fluid, and breast milk—play upon global infrastructures of sexism and make it seem as though women are not only just as likely but possibly more likely to transmit the virus than men, an assumption that simply isn't true. I noticed the ways that the virus, once considered a "death sentence," had made

a shift to "chronic illness," a shift that coincided with all the political issues surrounding Big Pharma and access. Most relevant to me became a cultural gap I recognized between those who had lived through the terror, fear, and confusion of the initial appearance of HIV&AIDS, the nightmarish loss of countless friends and lovers, the near decimation of a generation of young artists, and those who had grown up in a world with HIV&AIDS, learned about the virus in health class, knew it as a treatable disease, needed and wanted HIV testing to be more public and less scary. Simply a reality of their lived lives.

I stare at the postmarks, think about the dates. I consider the possibility, feel a promise for what's inside. I am overcome by the thought that these documents provide a direct connection to the past, a time before. Before my parents married. Before they had me and my brother. Before we moved from one house to another. Before my mother left. Before my parents divorced. Before my father came out. Before I came out. Before he contracted HIV. Before we knew anything about HIV or AIDS.

Sitting cross-legged, I place the ordered stack in front of me and begin reading. As soon as I see the second letter, one that began as an experimental drawing using reeds and India ink, I realize this is no usual set of missives. I open the next and the next and the next. I am stunned by their tonal range, the diversity of form. Each one, it seems, offering something different, something unexpected, something more. I take inventory.

In the twenty letters my father sends, he writes on twelve different kinds of "paper," including a cleaning cloth and a telegram. He sends the letters in eight different kinds of envelopes, many of which are adorned in cartoon drawings, covered in random last-minute messages. He writes the letters using nine different kinds of ink, including India ink; he employs ballpoint and felt-tip pens most of the time. He exhibits six or seven distinct types of handwriting, of which some might be described as bastardized cursive, some printing, most written using graphic back slant. In the twenty letters, he includes over fourteen different modes/forms of writing, including but not limited to his own poetry, philosophical statements, lyrical sentiments, rants, memories, humor, information, proclamation, confession. He incorporates a range of visual images and texts, including four different pieces of art, maps, and photographic images, and in one of the last letters, he tapes to the page a lucky penny he found that day, one he finds significant as it was minted the year of his birth.

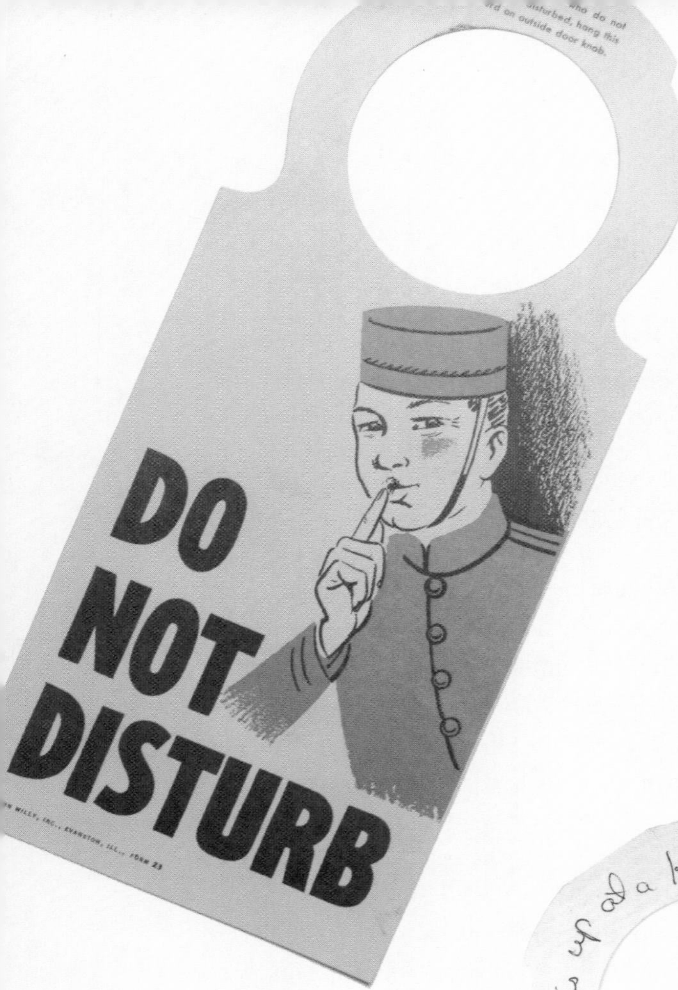
DO NOT DISTURB

20 letters

14 different modes/forms of writing

12 different kinds of paper

9 different kinds of ink

8 different kinds of envelopes

4 pieces of art

1 newspaper clipping

1 hotel Do Not Disturb sign

1 lucky penny

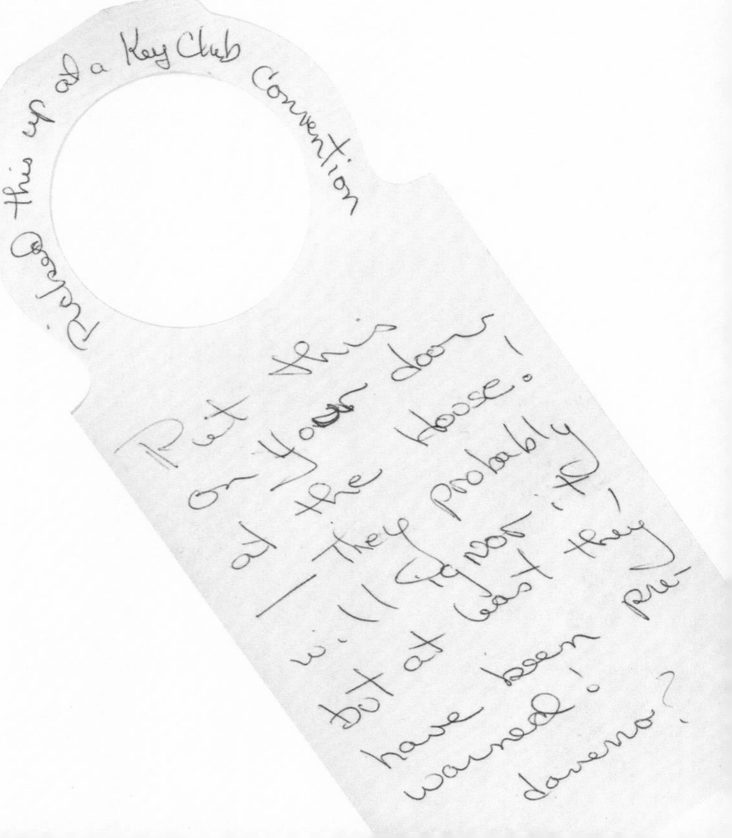
Picked this up at a Key Club Convention
Put this on your door at the House! They probably will ignore it, but at least they have been warned!

The letter is but one form, one genre, one way of writing. Yet the letter offers affordances other forms do not. In a letter you can write toward and for and to an audience of one. Be it a person (alive or dead), an idea, an entity, or even yourself, you are offered an occasion to write whatever and to whomever you wish. Certainly, a letter may be written to no one in particular, but the form itself invites the imagining of a recipient, an individual or even collective, that we hope will respond.

It is this imagined response, a desire for the mirrored writing of another, that intoxicates me. Letters provide us a way of placing all thoughts, sentiments, and ideas, both personal and political, in a form that shares with another the ways that we are able to communicate our interior lives. Letters enable us to share inner musings with ourselves.

I write letters to increase the intimacy I have with and for myself; to guarantee that I always have my own orifice—an aperture—an opening to/for/of desire. The letter's form is the means by which I open; the means by which I meditate and write. It is my way into a particularly personal relationship with language. It is how I have, since I learned to write, accessed my writerly desires, my authorial be-cummings.

In a letter, the greeting is the reader's invitation to pass through the orifice of the writer, through their fissure, a linguistic slit-as-letterbox accessible in their front door. It is permission granted to penetrate their words. Each greeting I think of as a particular set of labial lexicons, cursory curtains we often ignore, move too quickly past, worrying about getting to the body, the vocabulary to come (word choice I always want to cum), failing to realize that the body isn't yet to come/cum. We've greeted and opened, and so we are always-almost-already there.

In a letter, one is permitted to convert intellectual and emotional impulses into alphabetic text, position them all into what comes to be understood and felt as logical and orderly, regardless of how disparate and complicated the sentiments may be.

I write letters because I desire to write across forms, between genres; in all ways that call attention to gaps, fissures, interstices, spaces between and among feelings and thoughts. The form of the letter exists in a space of everlasting hope: for an understanding of self and the response of another.

I want to write in this manner because I not only hope but have faith in the way it generates openings between people, the creation of orifice for ideas, new ways of imagining scholarship as simultaneously personal and political, as always and ever erotic, as a connection between words through the clit and cunt; a connection that works in circular, reciprocal motion; pulsing, undulating, moving people, bodies, language, **desire.**

In high school, I was burdened by something I could not name. Different and yet similar to the cultural situation Betty Friedan identified in post–World War II America as the "strange discrepancy between the reality of our lives as women and the image to which we were trying to conform." Friedan named this image, this cultural narrative: the feminine mystique.

One might argue all teenagers are burdened by a discrepancy between a lived reality and image, a sense that they don't belong. I understood this, but I also knew my particular inability to fit in was somehow different. My struggle was connected to a disjuncture I could feel, from the inside out, with respect to dominant narratives regarding gender. I was battling a particular feminine mystique of my own. It wasn't about whether I had the right clothes but whether the "right" clothes were right on me. It wasn't about whether I could get boys to like me but whether I actually liked boys "in that way" at all. And, it wasn't about whether I marked the F or the M check box; it was about why there were only two boxes and that I would always have to think about it before choosing a box, be fine with choosing my legal letter, but I also always wondered: why do I have to choose at all?

I had lots of trouble sleeping: couldn't easily fall asleep; woke up multiple times every single night; lay awake for hours. This inability to sleep made me incredibly anxious, making it virtually impossible to relax. When it got really bad, I would look for one of my parents to talk with me. Most times, it would be my father. He was often still up anyway, watching TV, taking the dog out for a midnight walk to sneak another cigarette. Sometimes, because of his own neglect in placing a fabric order, he'd be working to meet a deadline for the interior design business he and my mother ran. He'd be making something that needed to be delivered the next day or should have been delivered the day before, something he'd refused to do, and so now he—rather than the drapery folks—was sewing someone's living room curtains in our basement, always without a pattern, most times without a plan.

My father had a short temper. Would scream at fabric. Would get angry with thread. Spit vitriol at the sewing machine. Curse his hands if they

made a mistake. If you approached him working in the daylight, he'd yell at you, too.

But, these late nights when I'd find him—whether it was 11:00, or 12:00, or 1:00, or 2:00—he would stop what he was doing to talk with me. In that same way people congregate at the best, most intimate parties, we'd move from wherever I found him in the house to the kitchen to talk. Sometimes I would sit on the counter and he'd stand. Sometimes he sat on the counter and I'd stand. Most times we'd both sit on the floor. He'd press his back against the stove, cross his feet at the ankles, and stare at his lap when I'd speak. When I listened to him, I'd count the slats in the kitchen closet louvered doors, compare the length of our legs, the shape of our hands.

The procedure was always the same: (1) Me: Identify an insecurity or injustice; (2) Dad: Actively listen; (3) Me: Emote; (4) Dad: Respond and support; (5) Me: Cry. Always cry. Then we'd remain on the floor for hours more. Shift into philosophical discussions regarding life. Grapple with the ineffable, the unknowable, and unnameable chasms I felt between being and self—between body and story, between space and time. For hours and hours, over the course of years, my father and I engaged in this process of communication, trying out and trying on ideas, sharing our personal perspectives during the wee hours of the night. So many hours spent talking with him, and yet I remember nothing of what he said. His interactions with me are impossible to categorize as fatherly advice.

What I do recall is the bodily sensation I had as we spoke. The visceral thrill incited by simply talking, moving from one word to the next. Rolling around together in ideas and words.

I read my father's letters searching for traces of our late-night revelations. I wanted to reconnect here on these pages the same way I once did on the floor, in the kitchen, in 1980. When I wore dresses and eye shadow. When my closeted interior designer father was married with children. When the art of conversation became conversation as art.

love

It's the reproduction of a cartoon my father includes in the fifth envelope, one postmarked September 8, 1966, that catches me in the diaphragm, causing me to punctuate aloud: "Oh. My. God."

adds a different twist to "who's in the closet?".

Did this a few years back — believe its a copy of something I saw….. !!!!

I stare at the drawing for a long time, considering the gaps, the spaces between. The juxtaposition between this image and the other contents in the envelope: a newspaper clipping from the May 14, 1962, edition of the Albany *Times Union* and a DO NOT DISTURB sign. The difference between the materiality of the pen and pencil; the aperture in time made manifest in the variance between the two mediums. The line drawn between "back" and "believe" in his comment on the cartoon signifying a pause in my father's thinking while writing. The distance between the irony of a closeted gay man including this cartoon in a letter to a woman he's trying to woo (a woman with whom he will, in a couple weeks' time, elope) and the "twist" my father can hardly predict. That he sends the cartoon to the woman with whom he will have two children, one of whom will be a female-born child who comes out first as lesbian, then later as a butch dandy transgenre writer, slices the taught surface of irony. But this is not all. A second twist ruptures wide the opening, revealing poignancy of ridiculous proportion. My mother saved the cartoon. And then gave it, tucked inside one of the letters, to me. It is now mine, this pre-me rendering. This image, a projection of his story-as-self: both here and not here. This reflection, a foreshadowing of my self-as-story. Let out of the closet. Lettered onto the page.

night is my favourite time of night
when the wind plays with my hair
and the moon chases the clouds.

What is it my father inadvertently let my mother see? Is it awareness of a public face, desire to be alone, affection for his own creativity, struggle with sexuality, the symbolism inherent in a newspaper clipping, a DO NOT DISTURB sign, a piece of a poem, this particular cartoon?

walk with me ——
on the street paved with marshmallow
                        dust
beside the chocolate stream

My father does as we all do in letters.

He lets my mother see these parts of him.

In doing so, offers permission as responsibility, as a kind of a lease; temporary, quasi-ownership of the parts of himself he finds most difficult to bear.

He reveals himself to himself, as he opens himself to her.

I think: *These letters are my blood.*

When darkness begins to shade
our cotton candy world
we'll sleep in the wind.

I can root myself here.

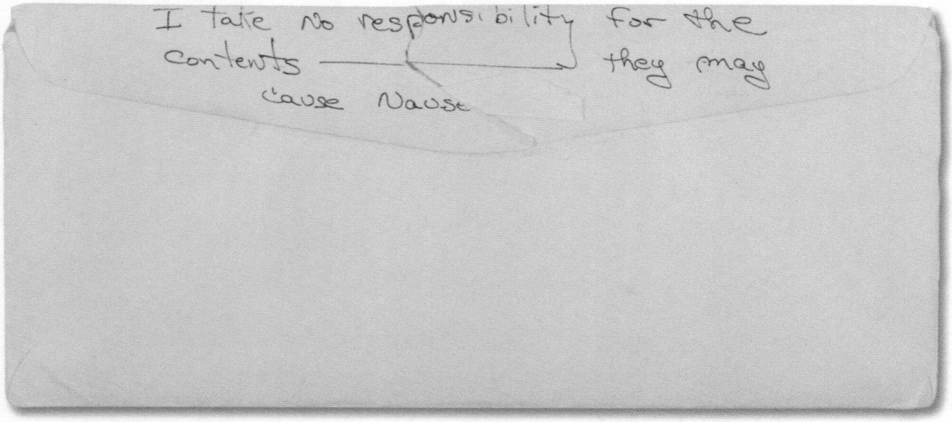
I take No responsibility for the
contents ————→ they may
cause Nause

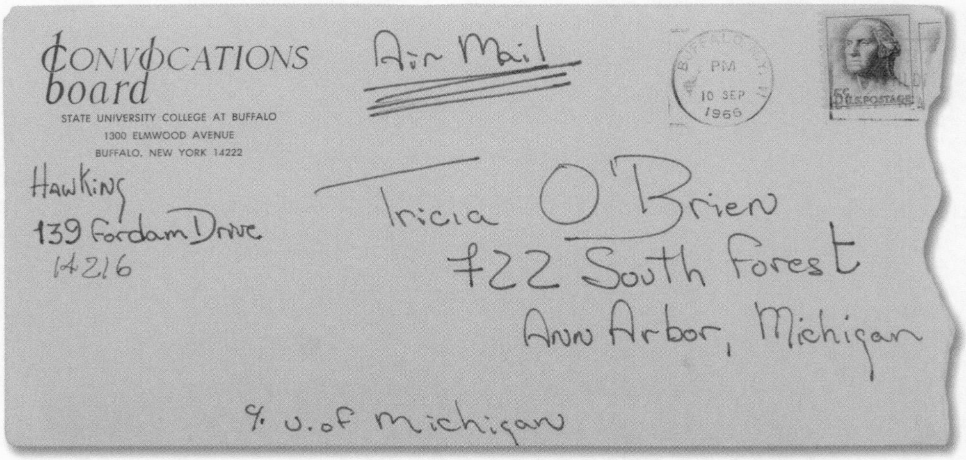
CONVOCATIONS
board
STATE UNIVERSITY COLLEGE AT BUFFALO
1300 ELMWOOD AVENUE
BUFFALO, NEW YORK 14222
Air Mail
BUFFALO N.Y.
PM
10 SEP
1966
U.S. POSTAGE
Hawking
139 Fordam Drive
14216
Tricia O'Brien
722 South Forest
Ann Arbor, Michigan
% U. of Michigan

BUFFALO, N.Y.
PM
10 SEP
1966

BUFFALO, N.Y.
PM
10 SEP
1966

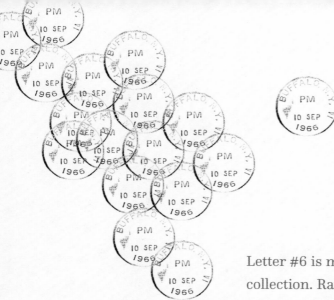

Letter #6 is my favorite in the collection. Rather than rip the envelope across the top seam, my mother tore this one down the right end, removing a slim sliver of paper no more than a centimeter wide. Even though I wasn't the one to originally create the tear, opening it—especially the first time—felt the way it did to unwrap presents when I was small, as though the act of ripping off the paper wasn't only about exposing the gift but about revealing the existence of magic itself.

BUFFALO, N.Y.
PM
10 SEP
1966

Placing the thumb of my left hand on the bottom edge and my fingers across the top of the envelope, I gently squeezed to create a vertical eye-shaped opening—an aperture—in the end. Peeking inside, I spied a particular shade of blue, a color my father refers to in the letter as "neet." While the color of the letter was both pleasing and unexpected, I registered actual surprise not with my eyes but through my hand. As soon as I pressed the "paper" between the thumb and forefinger, I could tell the material of the letter was not the smooth of pressed wood pulp, not stationery of the usual kind. Sliding it from the envelope, I stared at the folded rectangle for a while, turned it over in my hands before opening it, noting the translucence, the fabric-like texture, recognizing the substrate as similar to that of dryer sheets.

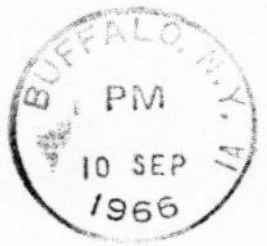
BUFFALO, N.Y.
14
PM
10 SEP
1966

I experienced a rush of breathtaking delight. My father had upped the ante, somehow topping his own choices for what counted as a letter-writing surface, shifting multiple times, in the space of two weeks, from India ink drawing, to telegram, to personal memorabilia, to this household item, a cleaning cloth. Had my mother not already been thinking the sentiment she's shared with me about why she was attracted to my father—*I'd never met anyone like him*—Letter #6 would have sealed the deal.

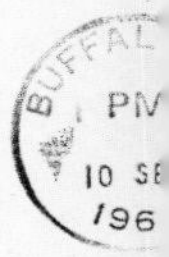
PM

Each time I unfurl this letter I see both the George who chose to write on the blue cleaning cloth in 1966 and the George who owned a Swiffer in 2008. I make a visual connection between the blue cloths that he and his friend Tom used to clean their apartment in Buffalo and the dry mop cloth extension pole I moved three times: once from an apartment into my house, once from my house into another apartment, once from that apartment into a senior apartment, the one that would be his last.

I am not at all surprised that my father was able to employ a delicate hand to maneuver the black felt-tip pen to craft the one-inch puffy letters on this thin, lacy surface. The shape, size, and spacing in and around these bloated letters make somehow more enchanting, more believable, this particular I LOVE YOU.

His proposal in the closing catches me completely off guard: "let's get married sometime we're in the same place for more than 2 hours."

Letter #6 enchants me because each time I remove it I know I'll spend as much time considering the blue cleaning cloth as I will reading the words. I'll stare at the luminous quality of the fabric, recognizing myself in the impulse to impress the one to whom I write, to imagine alternative writing surfaces, to turn my letters into art. Each time, I know I will fall in love with him just a little bit more, this man-who-was-not-then-but-will-now-become my father. Each time I become more grateful to my mother for saving and giving me the letters. Every time I read the letter, I stare at the tiny tangle of fibers on the fabric, hoping to see a way to love myself just a little bit more, too.

Written with the intention and hope for clarity, personal letters don't carry the burden of

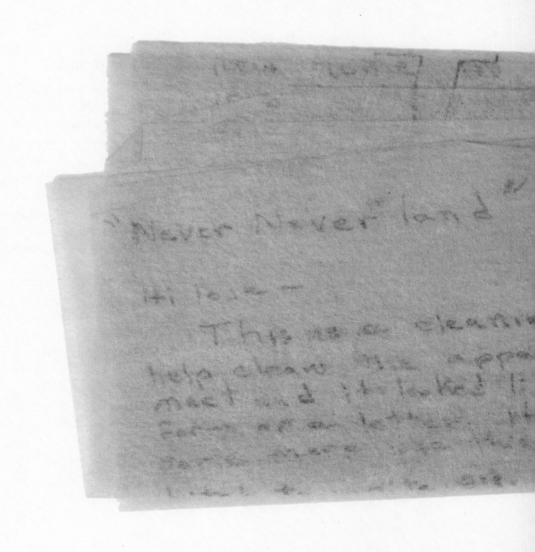

concision, efficiency, or linear logic. The goal is to reinforce or restructure a relationship; to offer

Babbette Hines opens *Love Letters, Lost* by explaining that her impulse to collect love letters was born in the space between "the stories we tell ourselves and the stories people tell about us." How do we represent ourselves to another person in writing? Are we truthful? How might someone receiving letters from us understand us, tell stories about us, and come to know us differently than one who never gets to see who it is we reveal ourselves to be in letters and language on the page?

I don't collect other people's letters in the same way Hines does, but reading them does feel something like collecting them. As though in reading what was once written by one person, and then held and saved by another, I am somehow now in possession of them as well.

But what is it that I actually possess? Is it the story? The sensation? Letter-ness? When I read do I come away with a better sense of the person whose letter I'm reading than I do its addressee? Why is it that in reading letters that have nothing directly to do with me I usually come away with a different, perhaps even deeper, understanding of myself?

One way to answer that question would be to think about which letters I choose to read and why. When I read letters that were not written to me, I read in search of the sensation of the writer, the reciprocal connection to a reader, the intangible magic of the space created that is always totally full of intention and words that could seemingly be produced forever. I read looking for the ways the writer works to bridge the distances—emotional, physical, narrative—that always exist between people, the ways the writer attempts to reach not only for the reader but for something just out of reach within themselves.

I may not have read all of the greats, or even any of the purported "greatest" love letters of all time, but there are some collections I've read in their entirety. Letters from Janet Flanner to Natalia Danesi Murray, from Vita Sackville-West to Virginia Woolf, from Emily Dickinson to Susan Huntington Dickinson, from Radclyffe Hall to Evguenia Souline, from Gertrude Stein to Alice B. Toklas, just to name a few.

an apology, condolences, thanks; to declare to a particular person, "I love you," whether using

It's immediately clear that my reading choices constellate around love letter exchanges between women, women who were also writers. Having been born female, socialized as girl and woman, and chosen most all of my life romantic and sexual relationships with other women, these are the stories and lives in which I have been most interested. In these missives, I feel the ways that the writers and readers experience both longing and loss, love of both flesh and syntax, an understanding of the letter as a genre of writerly possibility, as a generative opportunity to explore the work and wonder of words on a page.

In a love letter, the writer constructs a translated version of self, a revelation as an offering. The assumption is that the offering has been made at the pleasure of, with the love for, another in mind. This is both true and not completely true. As I read, I think about the relationships between Janet and Natalia, Emily and Susan, Virginia and Vita, Alice and Gertrude, John and Evguenia. And even as I read to learn about them, I am conscious of the ways I read in order to learn something about my writerly, woman-loving self. Their writing as a making, a reflection of who they are, their gender, and the assumptions about their own desires as well. My reading of their letters a practice of unmaking historical assumptions regarding sexuality and gender, the "true" nature of their desires as time may never tell.

Even when we work, in and with and through language, to do what we can to reveal, explain, and explore what we decide are our true feelings, our deepest thoughts, our most vulnerable selves, we can never be sure the person reading will understand what it is we have written, which truth—or truths—we do or wanted to believe, which ones we intended to articulate. We can hope to try to transcribe our "true" selves, can hope that the reader better understands our love for them and who we are, but the relationship is always asymptotic: we approach, and may nearly touch, but will never actually break this plane of knowing.

these particular three words in this precise order or not. Bodies of letters describe and inscribe

When Nina Sankovitch discovers a trunk full of old letters out in a shed behind the house she and her husband have just purchased, she immediately contacts her real estate lawyer to track down the sellers. She bought the house, but she didn't buy these. They needed to be returned.

It's likely that Sankovitch would have contacted the sellers and offered a return of the letters even without postmarks, the cultural marker of property. The inviolable sanctity letters achieve happens not only through a perceived protection provided by the U.S. Postal Service, but because of a transformation that has, prior to finding the letters, occurred. The letters moved from one person to another, across space and time. The letters were sealed with the intention they go only to the person to whom they were addressed. The letters must be prized possessions; they had been protected and saved.

Whoever letters they may have been—the woman to whom they were addressed, one Addie Seligman, or her heirs—what Sankovitch knows is that they are not hers. Not until the sellers make clear that they "didn't want the trunk or any of the stuff" that she found inside. Bequeathed by indifference after being found by chance, the letters become the starting place for her book *Signed, Sealed, Delivered: Celebrating the Joys of Letter Writing*, one woman's articulation of love for and fascination with the form.

I think about Sankovitch's response to finding the letters, her impulse to track down what we might understand as the "rightful owners." I consider how it would have been had my mother never given them to me and instead were I to find them after her death. I have the sense that if the letters were discovered far in the future, my future self would be interested

our most intimate connections. Not only those we have with each other, but the ones that we

in them to some degree, but I don't have the sense they'd so consume my time and attention. Maybe it's because I can't imagine that day. It seems so long from now. Maybe it's because, as I have quoted Clifford Geertz so many times, "Context is all," and without understanding the context of that moment, I can't say how it is I'd feel or what it is I'd do. But why, then, if I have no idea whether I'd bother writing about them as documents discovered in the future, does writing about them seem to matter so much now?

It is, I decide, precisely because the letters were directly given to me by my mother, rather than left to me to find, that I must write about them. Though the circumstances were different, Sankovitch and I both, in being gifted the letters, become another recipient in exchange; we exist as second iteration in transmission, another wave of movement for the letters across space and time. We are, via this transmission, not only permitted but invited—nearly required by its form—to read and respond. We could respond quietly, in our own homes, telling our response to another. But we are both writers. So, because there is no specific person to whom to write, we write not to the sender or the receiver. We write about them as a way to write about ourselves.

My gift feels more significant than that which Sankovitch received. I am in these letters. I am a part of their story. My existence foreshadowed on each page of prose. I'm not sure my mother was at all aware of how seriously I'd take the act of her giving me the letters, that I'd come to regard her handing them off as an opportunity to exhume a connection with my ancestry as writer. Dig for the treasured history of self.

have, seek, and desire with ourselves.

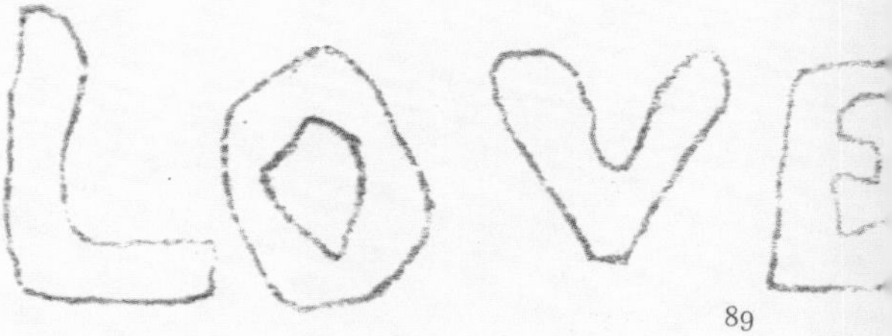
LOVE

k like I'm listening to what they're saying,
ng I'd like to do or something I'd like to

really tired tonight so I'm not going to
much more ————————————— but the day is
plete without talking to you. Every place I go
ly see something you'd like so I tell you abo
ill explain any unexplainable telepathic wav
d lately.

I LOVE y

(and I miss you terribly!)

let's get married sometime we're
the same place for more than

you're the best thing
in my life —

(do you object?)

all my love ————————
Giorgio

When I write a love letter, I begin
with the fullest intention of writing
to another person, a not-me with
a body of her own.

I open with Dear, or Dearest,
and then identify her by name.

I open my letter hopeful in/of expressing my desire:
to *be* with, to *speak* with, to *lie* with, to *feel* her.

I press fingers on pen or keys, and
offer my words as organs and limbs,
sentences as sinew and skin,
paragraphs as bone and blood.

I open each letter, always inspired
by body, writing for and to hers.

By the time I've fully entered the
body of the letter, the body I am
now writing (to and for) is often,
perhaps even usually, my own.

6 / September 10, 1966

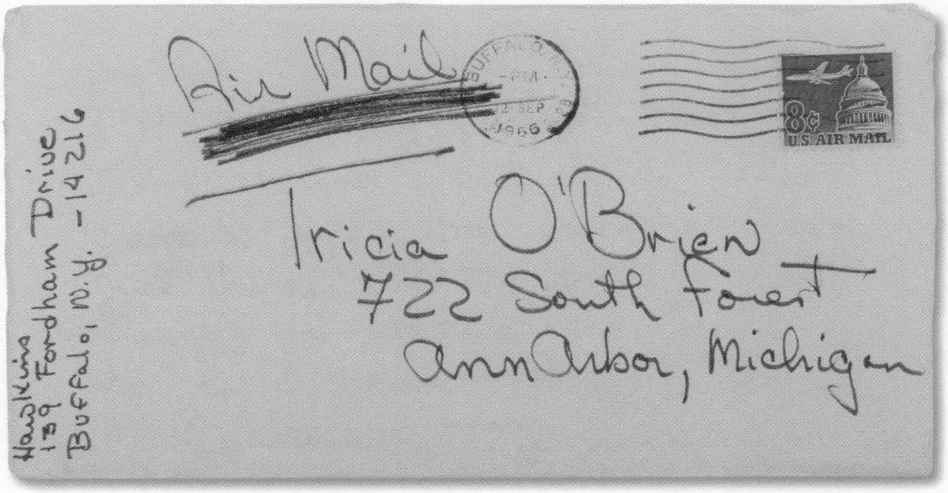
Air Mail
BUFFALO
PM
SEP
1966
8¢
U.S. AIR MAIL
Tricia O'Brien
722 South Forest
Ann Arbor, Michigan
Hawkins
139 Fordham Drive
Buffalo, N.Y. - 14216

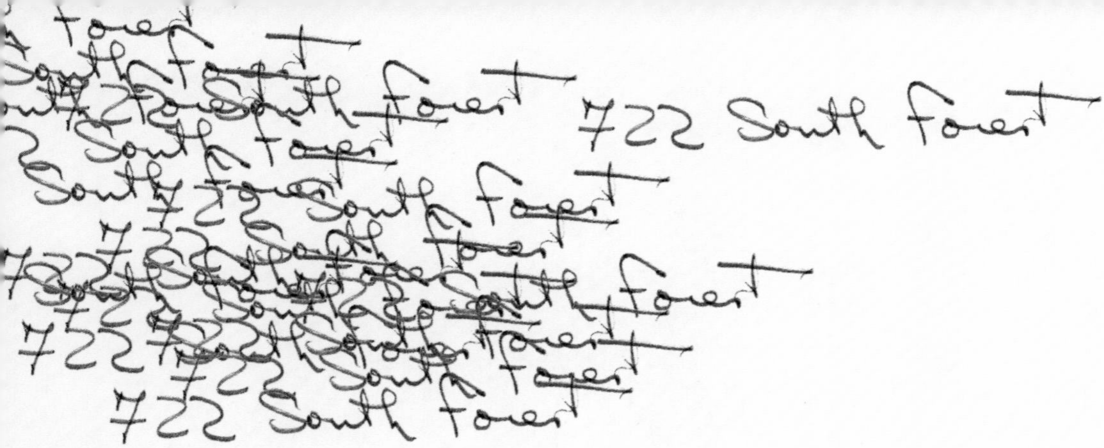
722 South Forest

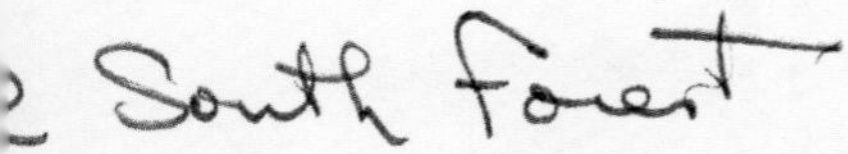

In 1966, my mother's birthday was on a Sunday. I imagine the weather as being perfect for the not-quite-mile walk from 722 S. Forest, the Beta Eta Chapter House of Alpha Delta Pi at the University of Michigan, to the Pretzel Bell at 120 East Liberty, a block from Main Street in downtown Ann Arbor.

Here, as was tradition for thousands of University of Michigan students during the course of the P-Bell's more than forty-year run, she went with her friends, in this case her sorority sisters, to celebrate her twenty-first birthday. My mother does not recall having done so, but newspaper articles offer that it was tradition for the celebrant to stand on one of the long tables and chug a pitcher of beer while the bar collectively sang "I Wanna Go Back to Michigan" and other drinking songs.

The beloved P-Bell closed two years before I arrived on campus, five years before I would join my Alpha Delta Pi sorority sisters in our adaptation of the "Bells" ritual. By 1990, we no longer went out for each and every sister's birthday. We would choose a particular day each semester to collectively celebrate all of the twenty-first birthdays that had transpired during the past few months. Each person participating in Bells had her own sponsor, usually her little sister. Same as was done in my mother's day, this woman would create for her big sister a bell-shaped poster on which were drawn either eleven or twenty-one lines. Eleven lines if you were drinking liquor drinks; twenty-one if you were drinking beer. Each woman "doing Bells" would hang the poster around her neck before embarking into the town to begin drinking in the later afternoon together, at some place like Goodtime Charlie's on South U, only a few blocks from the house. There was no real pressure to finish Bells, but there was honor in acquiring a complete set of signatures verifying completion of the eleven or twenty-one drinks.

love

I never received love letters at 722 S. Forest; I don't recall writing any from this address. This is, however, where I lived, one semester in a room called the Closet, with a woman to whom I for years after our college days wrote in and within love(d) letters. It's a place where I learned about Cixous's H, as Eta; that H sometimes begins with an E. It's the place where, separated by more than twenty years, my mother and I both lived as young women, an address we share as a once-upon-a-time home. It is a place to which I have little connection now, but when I read the letters my mother read in the same place I once lived, I locate my origins. At 722 S. Forest, I desperately sought to find something. In my father's letters to this address I begin to map out what it means to me to be where I am from.

THE
**STATLER
HILTON**
BUFFALO

Sunday
9/11/66

DELAWARE AVENUE at NIAGARA SQUARE • BUFFALO, NEW YORK 14240 • TEL. Area Code 716 856-1(

I love you Tricia —
It's too early to have
dinner or go out fresh

/ September 12, 1966

A Reading According to Sappho

On my blotter calendar,
with a mechanical pencil,
she wrote: John 3:15
"If you are not with me...," it warned.

She almost knew, I think,
with her creamy makeup
with her long hair
with her crisp enunciation
    with her sorority secrets
that I did not want to merely be with her.

In the dark, staring into chicken wire,
I picture clinging into her mattress.
In becoming the pea,
an annoying presence,
she'd have to feel.
Jesus-sputtered and truth-seeking
I find her one night,
after she found the Captain Morgan's
stashed in my desk drawer.
We drink until,
from the other side of the wall,
a screech insists on silence.
Muffled indignance exclaims
"I have a final tomorrow"
and thrusts us into my bed,
with buried faces, writhing bodies,
and convulsive laughter.

I began to realize that she could see,
    against the semigloss wall
      against old flannel sheets
        against cheap liquored breath
          against unknowable truth
that I was where I wanted to be: against her.

This is
This is the first almost-sex I ever had

love

He lies on the bed, on his back, head hanging over the foot, staring at the back of the chair pushed into the desk facing the wall. He listens. Hears his mother in the kitchen downstairs making his favorite steamed pudding. His brother out back playing with the dogs. His father in his study typing Sunday's sermon.

He's waiting. The wait before the beginning of school has always felt long, oppressive. It's hot outside, but this waiting is the kind he associates with the endlessness of winter. Waiting known as sameness, as snow stretched out across acres and acres of land; waiting as glacial, as sun glare that blinds but cannot melt. Waiting as endurance, as lifting and stretching; as hiking, as survival; muscle failure from no food. He's already waited by shopping, by getting his hair cut, by packing and organizing getting ready for school. Later, he might wait by reading or drawing. Right now, he's waiting by listening.

Just over a week ago, he hugged and kissed her goodbye. He said he'd write. And he has. Two letters the first two days he was home. And then, he stopped. Wanted to make sure. Wanted to know. Wanted to know what? Whether she'd write back? Whether she'd call? Whether she really and truly loved him, too?

And so, he waited. And they did talk. Twice! Still he thinks he should wait. But he wants to write her again. He wants to write her because he wants to feel. Because he feels this way. Feels as though all of life, everything, seems just beyond his grasp. Like the key to everything is waiting. Waiting is an activity that he understands. Something he's done a million times before. But right now, this waiting he is not quite sure how to do.

He crushes closed his eyes, sucks in a long stream of air past closed, gritted teeth. He flips over, first front to back, then around 180 degrees. Pulls a cigarette from the pack, lights it before lying back, smooshing his pillow beneath his head. He presses the tips of his fingers against his sternum, tries to touch the magnificent surges, riptides of emotion swelling and subsiding in continual waves, ones pulling hard back from shore and then decidedly crashing down around his heart. He swears he can feel her. Feel her feeling him. He feels only for this, only this feeling, this connection; only for talking with her.

He scooches up, looks down at his bare chest, drops the lit cigarette, and waits. Waits to know, to discover when it is he can get his skin to feel as much as his heart. Waits to see whether he's dreaming or awake. Whether he has died or is still alive. He watches as the bright cherry melts a hole in the tension, the surface of his skin-as-snow.

Reflexes suddenly kick in, and he snatches the cigarette from his belly and puts it out. He looks at the small circle of raw pink flesh, presses his fingers in toward the sides, noting how close he has to get before he can find pleasure in the numbness, joy in the pain.

He moves from the bed to the desk in one smooth stride, finds a piece of paper, stares for a moment. He doesn't have to think, doesn't even try. The words are there, and he opens: *Come vai mia ragazza?*

Waiting to write another letter, this is waiting he can control. Waiting, he realizes, he doesn't have to do.

It's shiny and gold-colored, covered with a symmetrical pattern suggestive of embossing, a box of unassuming size about nine inches long, five inches wide, two inches deep. One corner is torn, revealing the cracking gray of cardboard beneath the gold, an indication of its age, of my reliance on its purpose. Originally, this box held stationery purchased so that I could write thank-you notes for the gifts I received when I graduated high school. The box then traveled with me to college, where I discovered that the random thank-you note wasn't the only impetus I might have to move a pen across a page.

Over time, the contents of the box shifted from the empty sheets of heavy-weight unlined ivory stationery embossed with my initials to the letters I received from friends—some old and some new. I have two letters from my mother, two from an old boyfriend, a handful of postcards from a dear friend I made in graduate school, birthday cards given to me when I turned twenty-one, recent interaction with a friend newly rediscovered, and one sweet note from a young woman I used to babysit, sent when she was just twelve, a woman who now has children of her own, a woman I am proud to call my friend.

In addition to these missives is a set of communications that are the reason I continue to hold onto this box and keep safe these letters. Written to me by a college roommate, a sorority sister with whom I am now able to admit I once fell deeply in love, these epistles evidence our relationship, prove to me I wasn't crazy, that even if it wasn't exactly the same, she did love me, too. Her letters are mirror images of mine, linguistic reflections in reverse. Though I do not and cannot know exactly what I wrote (she has since thrown away my letters), I know my life and our communication dynamic well enough to recognize in her words that I came to sexual awakening through my own. Not ones that I cribbed, or borrowed, or mimicked, but the ones that were mine, words that I wrote to her.

Most of the letters are undated, and I could probably place them in order if I tried. Yet the historical record they present to me now, their content, is so much less interesting than the frequently repeated tropes indicating how the letter writing was important to her as well. I do not claim that she felt the same about me in terms of my longing, my desperate desire. I doubt she thought much about my penmanship, other than it was sometimes difficult to read, sloppy and unbridled, all chewy with consonant elision, fraught with misspellings. And yet her hand exacerbated my adoration for her crisp diction, her script so measured and neat, written always with fine-point pen, slender and deliberate. Her body was on the page for me, and I coveted this textual rendering. Most of her text remained light, a series of extremely well-written dapple-direct comments paired with recordings of daily life. She often acknowledged that she was confused by my philosophical musings, the inclination to see whether I could make language truly refer. She resisted my circuitous explanations, preferring the straightforward route, calling me on bullshit and challenging me to make sense, even as she chastised herself because she claimed to not.

As connected with the past as it may be, her prose bears witness to a relationship of depth, one of complex form. In rereading her letters I can recall the sensation, the compulsion to write her, to enter the space of composition and lust. I remember this time, before email and text, before a family and a career, when I would sit for hours, writing page after page, writing to her, yes, but also writing to myself. I wrote steeped in heartache, saturated in sorrow. Sometimes it was because of the relationship we shared, formed and bound by unrequited imperfection. But mostly I wrote because the letters let me live, allowed me to begin to see and understand what I truly desired. The way one might sit down with a tear-jerking movie, a song to help instigate tears, I would approach this writing, pining away for myself as much as for her.

She knew how much the letter writing meant to me, affirming my effort with simple declarations of delight regarding the attention I paid to the generation of words:

Wow, you sure know how to write a letter!

and

I was just thinking of you today and got home to find your letter in the mailbox.

and

So how's the summer treating you? Your last letter was intriguing—I read it like a five-and-dime novel.

Sometimes she goes further, as I most usually did, moving beyond plain appreciation, returning the desire to touch me with her prose:

Here I sit at the train station—been here for 45 min, have another 1 hour 40 min to go. I like people watching, but I don't want these folks to think I'm staring so what else is there to do besides drink beer at $1.50 a can? Why rummage through your luggage to find a writing tablet, that's what, and write to a long lost soulmate.

and

Your letter came just in time—"Calgon, take me away" without the Calgon. Funny how time is frozen when you read a letter. It's suddenly shocking to discover that a year has passed, especially when I think about how few times I've seen you. As I feel a boot at my backside and see reality ahead, opening up before me like an abyss, it sure is nice to know our friendship is constant. Like you said, that's really odd, I think. Soul mates.

Soul mates, we agreed, in letters and life. A striking statement for an exchange bereft of sexual innuendo, absent of directly carnal sentiment. None of these letters, not hers to me or mine to her, are explicitly sexual, yet I am now clear that I did use my words to make love to her. I learned the art of syntactical love making in the production of these letters. Before I understood what I was doing, could admit what it was, I came out and onto the page for her over and over again, using intimacy, rather than anatomy, as a way to reinforce relationship.

I know this because we eventually broke up, went our separate ways, providing finalizing confessions of love for each other through writing that ruptures wide. Her version, I am sure, is no less impassioned than whatever it was I once wrote to her:

It's all such a new feeling for me. You've taught me in many ways how to feel, how to express . . . but I sense that this time I'm learning a new feeling on my own—and at the same time I believe I never would have known this feeling had you not first taken me under your wing.

Do you know what I'm talking about? Do you feel it too? We may both have that same knot threatening to lodge in our throats, but they occur independently of each other; I am talking about the feeling of having a piece of your soul torn away, stolen, abandoning the rest of your soul. It seems as though we've shrugged off the thoughts of pushing or being pushed off the cliff, and instead opted to walk away from each other and climb down the opposite sides of the mountain. Certainly not a painless proposition.

Though it feels like you're ripping away from me now, I know it will always remain with me, in the best of my care, because I will never forget you.

Forget me not

I love you.

It is true. She has not forgotten me, and I have not forgotten her. It isn't possible. It isn't possible to forget someone with whom you have exchanged words such as these. It isn't because we remember the words themselves, remember exactly what was said. It's because we remember that words were shared, words born of body, birthed at the dawn of our adult lives. Words charged with love, and blistering honesty.

I, and all the women to whom I have since written, the lovers and friends for whom I consciously compose, have my correspondence with this particular woman to thank, this muse of flesh and verbiage who allowed me to sensually practice with syntax and sexually become in prose. And it cannot go without saying that I also have to thank her for keeping my history, as she, not I, ultimately marks my coming-out, sets for me an awakening, a date to which I often feel unable to commit, ever reticent to decide when the words came, which ones were important, which ones I will use. Fittingly so, she provides evidence in words; a poem from her, a gift for me, lovingly crafted on off-white, textured card stock, featuring a hand-painted lavender lambda, written in six different colored pencils, sent to me in the spring of 1993, reflecting back to me my own struggle.

Ironic, one might respond, to hear me claim that the actual poem, the words she wrote, doesn't matter now. As peculiar and paradoxical as it might be for me to claim that these words are irrelevant—to be sure, I have argued most assiduously regarding the difficulties I faced when I have been bereft of language—I claim only that these particular words (not words themselves) are immaterial. They are extraneous because knowing these words, knowing what she said to me most precisely, has nothing to do with what I now know. What I know about sex or anything else isn't about having the words, exacting vocabulary with fastidious definitions. It isn't about precisely what was said, how it was relayed. This kind of knowing has to do with using words, with letting them and lettering them, in positioning them for each other and ourselves.

> To let her live.
>
> To let her love.
>
> To let her.
>
> To letter.
>
> To let her letter.
>
> To matter.

love

THE
STATLER
HILTON
BUFFALO
BUFFALO TO:
CLEVELAND - 197 Miles
NEW YORK - 420 Miles
TORONTO - 100 Miles
MONTREAL
TORONTO
Niagara Falls
BUFFALO
ALBANY
BOSTON
DETROIT
CLEVELAND
NEW YORK
BUFFALO World Port of Progress and Pleasure

7 / September 12, 1966

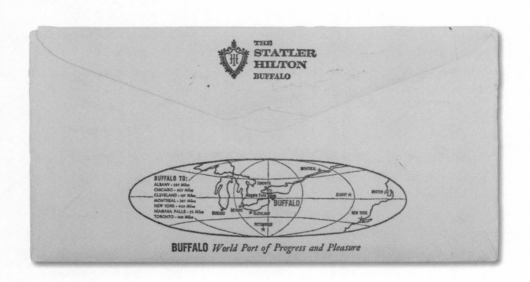

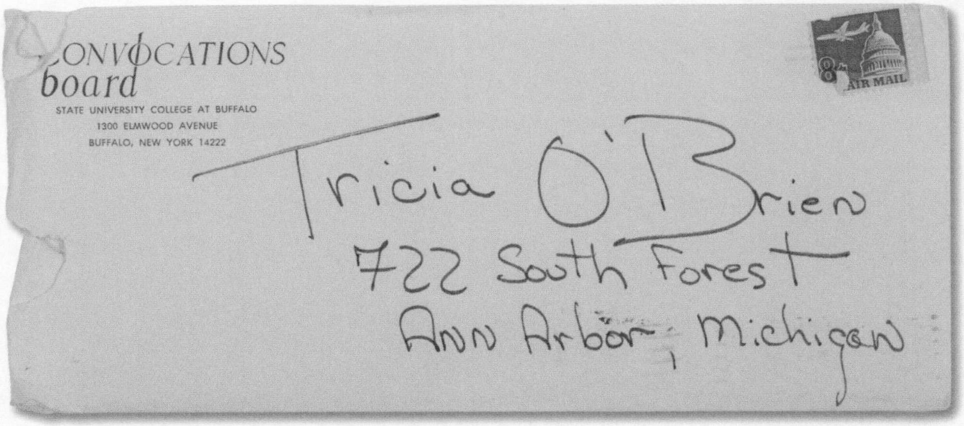
CONVOCATIONS
board
STATE UNIVERSITY COLLEGE AT BUFFALO
1300 ELMWOOD AVENUE
BUFFALO, NEW YORK 14222
AIR MAIL
Tricia O'Brien
722 South Forest
Ann Arbor, Michigan

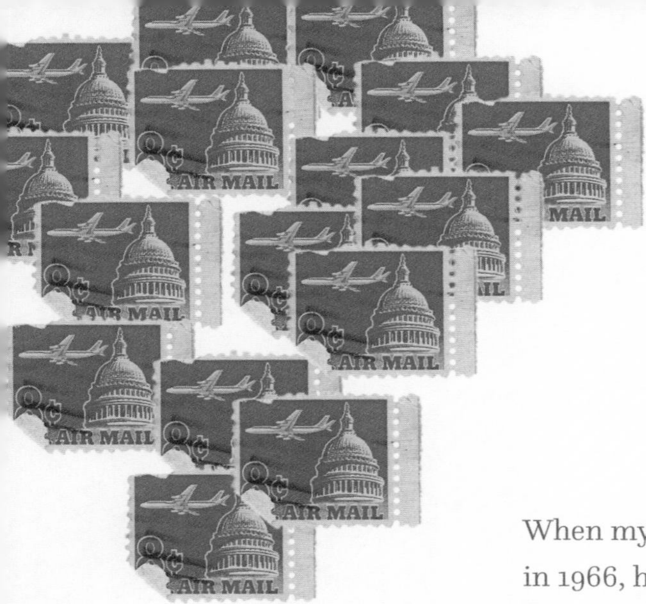
AIR MAIL

When my father bought stamps in 1966, he was paying nearly the same rate for postage that people had been paying one hundred years before. Standardized in 1863, a rate of three cents would purchase transmission of a half-ounce letter; by 1932, that same three cents afforded you transportation for a full ounce.

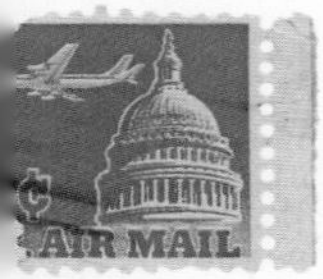
AIR MAIL

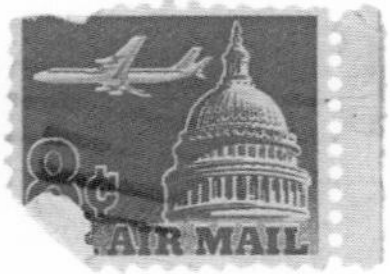
AIR MAIL

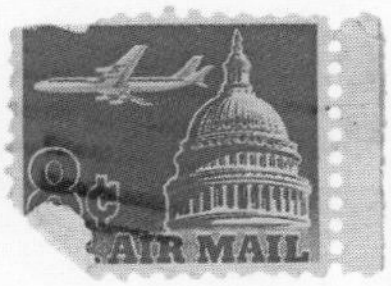
AIR MAIL

It's the twenty-cent stamp of November 1, 1981, that I first recall, the one with the larger full-color American flag on a white field flying over a black line drawing of the Supreme Court. Thank-you notes and letters from camp were likely all I was writing then, but I have a clear memory of going into my mom's desk drawer to find what felt to be the never-ending roll of stamps secured inside a pewter dispenser. There was a little knob at the top I'd turn to make them magically appear, and I loved carefully counting the number of stamps I'd need, watching for the correct line of circular perforations before folding and gently tearing downward, removing the crisp, official-looking white strip.

In my house, letters were sacrosanct. More than communication, they were understood as personal possessions, the private property of the person to whom the letter was addressed. This status as sacred, I realize, was in part created by the commonly held belief that it was not simply unethical but illegal to open the mail of another person.

I was told that you could go to jail for opening a letter not addressed to you.

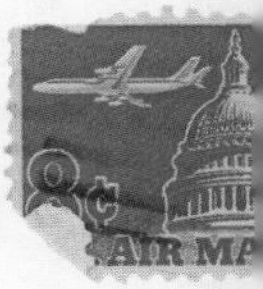

I love thinking about the fact that Emily Dickinson, who, though she lived next door to Susan Huntington Gilbert Dickinson, wrote letters to her nearly every single day. Historians argue about whether Emily was a lesbian. I believe that such a label is irrelevant, immaterial, and entirely beside the point. All letters materialize the act of reaching out, reaching forward and toward another, with writing. We extend ourselves, through our hands, sometimes in our own hands, as ideas conveyed through language, onto the screen and page. The love letter differs only in intention, in degree, in the depth of the relationship one seeks.

That the love letter is about relationship is not in question. But this relationship, I'd argue, isn't always only one we seek to have in the flesh, with another person. What's interesting and somewhat unusual about Emily's letters is that they are, as many might argue, over the top. They're packed with sticky-sweet overwrought sentences and sentiments. They are, as my father would have said, "too much." What if Emily wasn't writing to Susan to convince her of her love, but because she loved the way it felt to write, to be in love with language on the page? What if writing wasn't about loving Susan, but about simply loving what it felt like to grow to know and love her own writerly self? Though Judith Thurman doesn't make too much of this idea, her observation in the *New Yorker* regarding

Dickinson's poetry stops me dead in my tracks: "Few voices are more solitary than her first person, yet few are more intimate: she writes I to I."

Yes, I think, this is it. How else to perfect this voice than to write to herself, for herself, through and to Susan, this woman whom she adored? The love letter may not always be used to its fullest potential, but the form provides one the possibility of using writing to discover and explore language as love both of and perhaps even as self.

Was my father, then, only writing to himself? Not on purpose, I would argue. His twenty-one-year-old self surely believed he was writing to someone he loved. And yet I am so very aware that when I write a letter to another, I am also engaged in a conversation with myself.

Love letters let go: they letter vulnerability. They evidence desire not only for another but to expose interior longings and thoughts unseen. Perhaps we collect letters, desire to manifest collections of love letters, because whether conscious or not, through their repetition and accretion they show us that we have the power through love as/ and/with language to shape and change our own worlds. To craft narratives of a self who loves, who has loved, and is able to love herself as much as she loves another, a self that she adores when she writes I to I.

on a sheet of paper and
e pleased. was glad to
that you get in moods &
s of disconnected thoughts
no one ~~that~~ seems to
stand but the self ———
there are 2 of us that
ow of & that is ENOUGH
nat little book is so
ifull ——————— the author
got to be one of the
st people alive ——— either
or he met us and did bothe
troduce himself. You're so
for sending it & "I luvs ya
t!"

love

When I wrote to my friends in the 1990s, I was lost in the content of my letters, self-absorbed in my own identity-crisis moment. I was struggling with language, the words for the deep-body knowledge I had regarding both my sexuality and my gender. I was consumed by what was often the desire to communicate my love for women who did not love me in the same way. Always worried about what I was trying to say, and I was trying to say "I love you" in every other way than just saying it. I remember attempting to be as indirect as possible, working language and sentences, massaging grammar and syntax, all to skirt my feelings, yet place enough energy out there to solicit a response.

Long before I ever knew about the letters that moved between my parents, I was interested in the point and purpose of letter writing for writers, poets, and artists. I asked my friend whether she'd kept any of the letters I'd written to her. Before I identified deeply with, and in, my own realms of sexual and syntactical desire, she responded thus:

> *I look back with embarrassment. I am embarrassed at my other extremes: the excessive drinking, the excessive "whatever" attitude, the excessive need to be found attractive by boys, etc. I wince when I remember specific instances of my own stupidity. Maybe that's why I eventually threw out the old letters—they served not only as a reminder to me of what a lost person I was, but as a record of it all for the rest of the world. Imagine my kids reading them! Imagine them being dug up and published a hundred years from now! Egad! The thought is too much to bear.*

> *You, on the other hand, save the letters and admit that the romantic idea of our relationship was better than the gritty reality borne out by them, but maybe it's more that our friendship was a constant respite from the gritty reality . . . that we were friends despite and because of our differences. The letters bear witness to the fact that in spite of all we are and*

all we aren't to each other the friendship remains constant. Comforting and mysterious, isn't it?

What strikes me most when I read her response is that the letters she threw out are the ones I wrote to her, even though I likely did not write about whatever she perceives as her "instances of stupidity." I would have written about my own. But this means that though they are from me, it is her self—not me, not mine—that she finds embarrassing. A self she found reflected in words I wrote to and for her, the self that she once presented to me, the one from which she now seeks distance.

This is distance she needs to preserve because even though neither of us was or is famous, her letters are still around. She's aware that there's always the possibility that the letters may be "dug up and published a hundred years from now! Egad!" Yet, I would never breach this confidence, never offer them to her children to read. Not only because I honor this indirect request, but because, as she points out, I am always somewhere in the letters she sent to me, a self I save less to remember than to re-create.

Because the fact is that I am equally embarrassed by my past when I read her words. I recognize love unrequited, feel my longing for something I believed impossible then: acceptance as a romantically lovable, sexually desirable person. Her words offer a return to a time of desperation, a great flailing, and I cringe. But my impulse isn't to destroy, to dispose. My instinct is to hold on until I can remake, revise, recast. I accepted her words as an artist, saved them as medium. Letters with words made of letters from which I can make different words recorded in new letters.

I save letters because I write letters. I write letters so that I may come to know myself as words. It's a constancy I find both "comforting and mysterious," indeed.

The popular myth that it's illegal to open the mail of another person in any circumstance stems from the fact that it is illegal for any person to tamper with mail at any point it is in possession by the U.S. Postal Service. Initially written in 1940, Title 18, Part I, Chapter 83, Section 1702 of the U.S. Code states:

> Whoever takes any letter, postal card, or package out of any post office or any authorized depository for mail matter, or from any letter or mail carrier, or which has been in any post office or authorized depository, or in the custody of any letter or mail carrier, before it has been delivered to the person to whom it was directed, with design to obstruct the correspondence, or to pry into the business or secrets of another, or opens, secretes, embezzles, or destroys the same, shall be fined under this title or imprisoned not more than five years, or both.

The relevant clause here, buried in the middle of this paragraph, is this: "before it has been delivered to the person to whom it was directed." So, you can't mess with the mail in any way, for any reason, when it's understood as being the temporary property of the U.S. Postal Service: in a mailbox, the official blue ones or your own, in the hands of a postal carrier, in a mail truck, in the post office itself. Should, however, the letter safely arrive at its projected location, in the residence where the intended recipient still resides, said letter no longer receives protection by the U.S. government. Anyone can, legally speaking, at any time prior to or following a letter's official time with the Postal Service, open and read it.

So why do we believe, despite the fact that it's clearly stated, that this protection extends beyond the scope of the statute? To begin, it appears we internalize the Postal Service as somehow connected to our freedom of speech, the right to speak with whomever we want, however we desire, without threat of anyone taking our words, stealing our secrets, slandering our reputations. Through the technology of the stamp we not only purchase transportation for our postcard, letter, or package, but also contract some kind of protection of what we understand to be our property, this thing/ object that we've created, our thoughts and words expressly intended for, only to be seen by, one other person. We think, in other words, of the postal statute as being, like the service we purchased, in place for us as letter writers, not necessarily as protection for the government to safely transport our mail.

But there's something else of relevance here, something less a part of economics and contracts, having more to do with the movement of letters across time and space. What happens in the transmission of letters is what confers upon them their sacred quality. The time a letter spends with the Postal Service becomes a mechanism of transformation. It's a liminal space whereby the document shifts from being property of the writer to property of the intended recipient, the addressee. First, the person writes a letter, enters a kind of sacred space, brings to the fore the object of their focus, creates for another a piece of themselves on the page. In this letter, we feel and know some piece of our selves; this writing is an extension of us.

Then, by subsidizing its travel, we entrust the government with temporary possession of not just our communication but, especially in the case of a love letter, a piece of who we are, who we want to be with, who we endeavor to become. We make a conscious choice to send our composition of self on its way by putting it in a mailbox, handing it to a postal carrier, or taking it to the post office proper. No longer in our hands, both not and yet also still ours, it is sorted, transported, delivered. Stamped and postmarked, the letter bears the symbolic layering of its own private initiation rite, moving, often literally, from one state to the next, one person to another. This movement through time and space, our words, this part of who we are, entrusted to government, contracted by economic exchange, reinforced by their safe arrival, now becomes, as intended, the property of, the possession of, an offering to our specific intended other. This is a letter. And an official document. It is us on the page as gift.

Most times when I slide a letter into a mailbox, I do so in earnest, with confidence. The letter has been written with a specific addressee in mind, with the complete trust that the letter will arrive at its destination. Even more, I usually do so with the sense that my communication, when it arrives, will be both welcomed and read by the addressee, my intentions clearly understood. I don't usually think about the possibility that the letter may not arrive, that it could be misdelivered or determined undeliverable. I place a return address on most all of my letters and am usually confident the one to whom I'm writing still lives at the indicated address. In other words, I feel fairly certain that letters I send won't end up in the Mail Recovery Center, what we used to call the Dead Letter Office, where letters are opened by someone else looking for a return address, some way to move the letter either backward or forward in the intended, presumed closed, circulation route.

More than halfway into the writing of this project, I realize that the confidence I have about a letter successfully getting from one place to another reflects a similar surety regarding my interpretation of the power and meaning not only of love letters, but of particular narrative scenes regarding my parents' courtship and marriage. In none of what I offer here in these pages do I ever mean to misrepresent my parents or their lives. I have done what I can to gather and relay as many facts as I could. Yet I recognize that when I opened and read each of the letters my father wrote, I was not doing so looking for details to move them forward on their way to their intended destination. I was looking for a way to make sense of where I had come from. The letters my mother handed me were not dead. The letters, that narrative, had already arrived.

However, when she gave them to me they were, in a sense, resuscitated. New breath pushed into these old letters reveals a new opening. This is what I learn: What it is I think I know about my parents and their relationship, though connected with and to fact, is fated to be inaccurate even when it may be honest. Any truth in this book is always-only connected with and to my own life.

Tricia

8 / undated

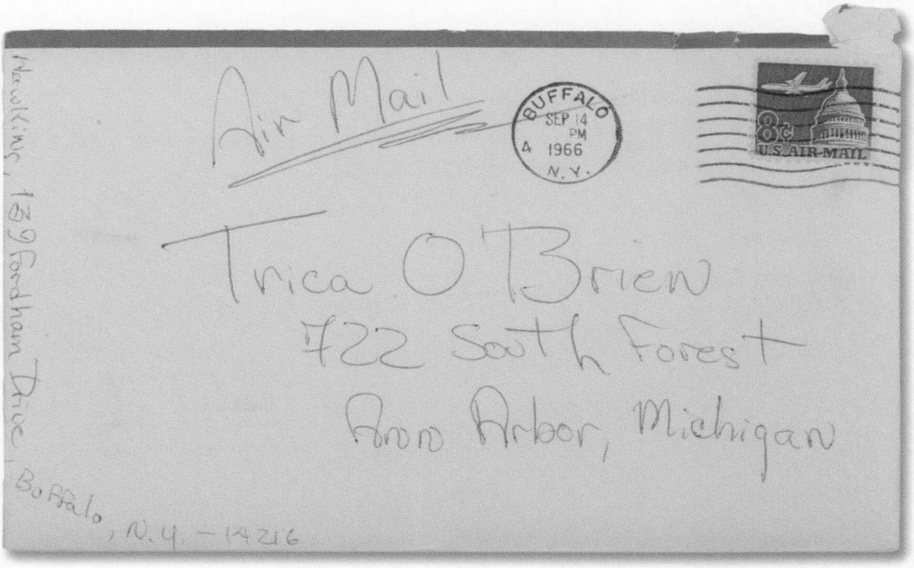
Air Mail
BUFFALO SEP 14 PM 4 1966 N.Y.
8¢ U.S. AIR-MAIL
Trica O'Brien
722 South Forest
Ann Arbor, Michigan
Hawking, 139 Fordham Drive, Buffalo, N.Y. – 14216

By the second time I read the letters,
my father is dead.

I arrive at a writers conference in Banff, Canada, two years after reading the letters the first time. Sitting in the hotel room alone, using the second bed as a table, I lay out the letters in a grid, first four rows of five, then—because I don't quite like how it looks—five rows of four.

As I move across the rows, left to right, I start to think about each letter not only by its postmarked date, but as a number. By Letter #14, I'm starting to skim rather than read. I become simultaneously bored and fascinated with the process of opening and reading, compelled to keep repeating the motions, opening and looking, moving through them faster and faster. Each one is unique, but together they are now a collection, dependent upon each other for the logic of the whole.

I keep thinking: *There's no there there*. They are, collectively, a kind of textual ouroboros. Self-consuming, they are always both full and empty. Each is always both more and less than the one that came before. I had intended to spend all day with the missives, and instead I've blazed through them all in an hour and a half. I stare at the matrix on the bed and wonder: *What the hell am I going to do now?*

what is going through
our minds.

Tricia ——→ I love you!

giorgio

Love letters afford the means by which it is possible through both creativity and passion, both

9 / September 14, 1966

What does it mean for a truth to always be present even as it remains unseen? As far as love letters go, these writings are fairly chaste. And yet they are full of lust and longing: raw, untamed desire. Each letter is both unique and similar; twenty iterations of the same idea: the pronouncement that my father knows nothing other than his desire for painting, for art, the oft-repeated declaration: *Giorgio is/I am in love with you.*

Snow crunches beneath my feet as I walk and think about my father's hands. His agents of making, of marking and word crafting, the repetition of writing and doing, the time and attention he gave to each page. I become acutely aware that it isn't only his making of these missives that matters, but my mother's unmaking of them, the movement of her hands in opening envelopes and removing each page. She in reading, decoding, and saving them has made possible their survival. She, the appreciator of writing, of him and his art.

I stop in the snow and raise my hands, look down at my feet and consider the space between. Suddenly, I burst. Explode into a short series of sobs. Four, maybe five heaves, similar to those I released over the body of my father after he died. My brother recently recalled the moment when Dad died as "when you completely lost it." I reminded him that my reaction lasted less than six seconds. "Yeah," he said, "but that was so unlike you."

intellect and romance, both intimacy and cunning, to explore a relationship with ourselves and

My childhood home is my ontological center; the city in which I was born and raised, my epistemological hub. Even though we didn't officially move there until I was nine, I am from Grosse Pointe; I am of it. I was born in Bon Secours Hospital, educated in the Grosse Pointe Public School System, graduated from Grosse Pointe South High School, was a chorister at Christ Church, Grosse Pointe. I can get you to almost any address in the Park, City, or Farms, and I can still, on any given day of the week, at any time of the year, walk into the Village and, though I haven't lived there in more than twenty years, in less than half an hour run into at least one person that I know, that knows, or knows of, me. I believe that football games are to be played in the daytime, that a martini should always be dry. I prefer the smell of the lake in the morning, grass clippings in the afternoon, leaves in the evening, and snow in the dead of night. And, I know about fish flies, what it feels like to have them pop under your bike tires, to have to be very careful about stopping at the bug-covered corners as the streetlights bring the mouthless winged-ones by the thousands, tiny carcasses on the pavement as slippery as leaves in fall.

My hometown is the hometown of fictional characters such as Maggie O'Connell, the sassy bush pilot in *Northern Exposure*, Martin Blank, the hired assassin in *Grosse Pointe Blank*, and, more recently and obscurely, the hometown of Rita Bennett, serial killer Dexter Morgan's murdered (but not by him) wife on *Dexter*. These characters' shared background

another through language. In reading the letters written by others, ones never intended for us,

creates for each of them conflict between the implied childhood experience and their adult choices. In other words, they were Grosse Pointers who didn't specifically and directly reflect the beliefs, values, and mythologies that undergird and guide this old WASPy town. The story here isn't that being from Grosse Pointe can lead you to choose a strange, alternative career. The tension is created by the unlikelihood that someone from such a stable, predictable, clean-cut, white bread, well-bred community would ever choose these sorts of occupations/partners in the first place. It's the juxtaposition with Grosse Pointe aesthetics and sensibilities—the friction—that creates narrative interest.

I feel and use the Grosse Pointe privilege that often doubles as baggage when I either proudly or hesitantly state where I am from. I am embarrassed by its history of racism. I acknowledge the opportunities that growing up here allowed. My brother is equally at odds with his origins, but for different reasons. His choice to live in a smaller, and by my standards rural, city in Illinois makes him hesitate to connect himself with a place that would never allow him to line up three or four riding mowers in the backyard, to have a truck on blocks in the driveway, to run a log splitter for two, or six, or ten straight hours in order to cut and stack cord after cord of wood to heat his home by wood-burning stove. Yet, I love this place because Grosse Pointe is the thread that binds our family. I am always both from here and not from here, located in a place, even as I often feel as though I am from nowhere at all.

we are in our reimagined ownership, learning more about how we tell stories. In reading these

We are instructed from a young age to recognize value in lineage, to see ourselves as the next chapter in a particular familial story, one often beginning with us, moving backward to our parents, to their parents, to those who begat them, and all those who were previously begat. Repeatable stories constructed from whos, whens, wheres, and whats fashioning relevance for our lives. These grandparents, those surnames; this farm, that city; this ethnicity, country, town. Identity established through comparisons of hair and eye color, strength of hand, shape of face. Who are you most like? Whom do you resemble, favor, take after? Whom would you have liked had they still been alive? Who laughs, feels, walks, talks, speaks, runs, smiles, looks most like you?

Perhaps this is why it always feels transgressive, even unethical, when I say: "My parents were both adopted." This isn't my story my mother made clear when I was seven, when I tracked her index finger as it moved from images of her pregnant to images of teeny tiny me: "No, you were not adopted. I gave birth to you."

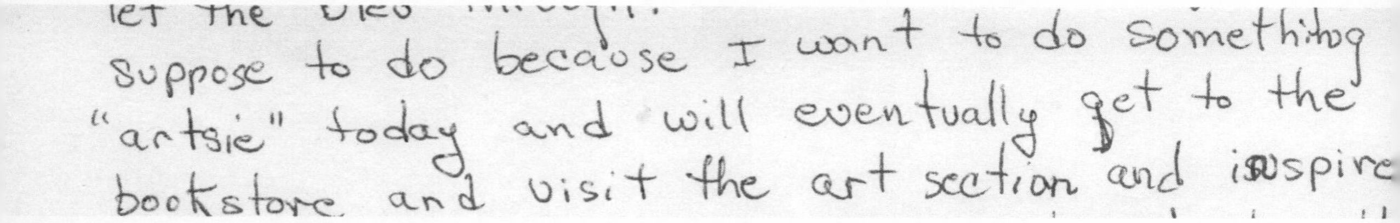

let the video interpret.
suppose to do because I want to do something
"artsie" today and will eventually get to the
bookstore and visit the art section and inspire

letters, we craft collaborative legacies both on and off the page.

Here,

I say, *this is where I am*

from. I stretch flat my left hand,

knuckle-side up, use the right index

finger and point to the ridge, the place about

an inch below where the carpal and meta-

carpal of my left thumb meet. To some it looks

as though I've just pointed to a nothingplace on nowhereskin.

To those who speak MI language, I have just located home.

I am from the American Midwest, where we put prepositions at the

end of sentences and purposefully nothing-place our language

over and over until it runs out of room, until it becomes all the

space we need to move.

I am from the lower peninsula of Michigan, and I carry   my map

with me. It is on my hand. It is in my hand. It is my   hand.

I am from Grosse Pointe Park, Michigan, where I learned to read and write. In

red-brick buildings full of wood and white trim, lined with privilege and pride.

I am from an address where my mother showed me language as love,

the life-giving power of reading and books.

I am from somewhere because my parents were from nowheres

and nothings.

I am from city as story, language as law, heritage

as narratives.

I am from love letters as land and writing as roots.

From the moment we moved to Grosse Pointe, I was taken with the sidewalks. Not because I had never seen one before, but because these sidewalks were different. Sidewalks in Grosse Pointe didn't simply sit out in front of houses the way I had seen in so many Detroit suburbs, circling the block like a go-cart with a list. These sidewalks actually went places, to the Village and the Hill, to school and church. They led me to something I wanted to see, buy, or do. These sidewalks were wide. Two kids could ride down the sidewalk side by side; three kids could walk abreast without anyone having to step on the grass. As a series of clearly standardized squares, they were graciously broad, gracefully level, and even in grade. A patchwork of materials and a collage of wear patterns, the squares revealed the relative age of the community. The eldest squares were single stone pieces, flagstone or slate. The older concrete pieces were darker in color, dotted with pebbles and rocks, pocked with pits where the stones in the concrete mix had, due to years of weathering, broken free. The newest squares were smooth, white, and perfect, save for an occasional dog paw print, stick drawing, bicycle tire track, outline of a leaf.

I cannot think about the sidewalks in Grosse Pointe without thinking about the stamps left by J.J. Barney Concrete, dog-tag shapes that appear randomly, yet predictably, every few concrete squares or so. My friends and I used these markings to play a variety of hopscotch-like games. We'd race from "J.J. Barney" to "J.J. Barney," slamming our feet down upon the indentation as if we were simultaneously running to first base. Other times, we'd try to leap from "J.J. Barney" to "J.J. Barney," doing whatever we could to try to not step on any other bit of concrete. Sometimes we would play a kind of hunting game, sprinting from marking to marking, trying to find the oldest year we could: *Here's '78, oh wait, '77! I've got 1967. Oh, look,* and we'd stop and stare with reverence and say together, *Oh my God, it's 1926.*

Grosse Pointe is my home, my somewhere. It is a guidepost, a compass, a map that provides a way for me to make sense of life. Grosse Pointe is my sidewalk. The way I use my body to navigate from one place to the next, negotiating between order and chaos, foundational to an endless journey embarked to discover where I may best exist.

My father's adoption story wasn't ever hidden, but it also wasn't ever told with as much joy. My mom reports that Grandma Betty, my father's mother, used to tell it this way.

> Ellen was beautiful and perfect and born dead. The doctor said that it would do me some good to get a baby for the holidays, something to cheer me up. So, we drove the few hours to the Catholic orphanage. I wanted a baby girl, an infant, and asked for one. Instead, they brought me this little boy. Well, he was nice and sweet, and I played with him for a bit. But, then I said again that I was here for a baby girl. They took George away. I waited for what seemed like forever, asking whether I could see a baby girl, and they smiled and said they would see what they could do. A little while later they came back in with George. By this point it was late in the day, and I realized that I was going home with him or I was going home empty-handed. So, we took George home. He was supposed to go back after the holidays, but I wouldn't return him. He was cute and fun and, I decided, even better than an infant because he could do so many things.

While that should have been that, there was a hitch to the story: my father's birth mother had never officially signed off. He wasn't eligible for adoption. As a result, my dad was driven back and forth to the orphanage every six months or so for the next couple years for visits requested by his maternal grandmother. Betty and Bowen Hawkins became foster parents for my dad and began putting pressure on my dad's mother to finally sign papers releasing him for adoption. When my dad was three, his mother signed whatever papers were necessary. George was officially a Hawkins by the time he was four.

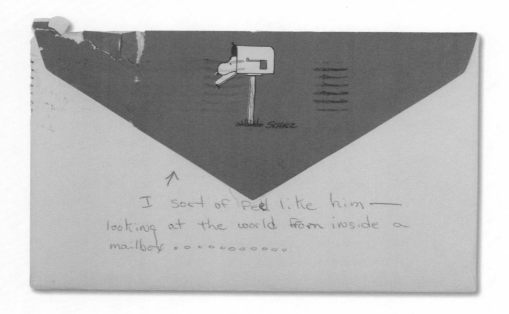

I sort of feel like him —
looking at the world from inside a
mailbox . . . .

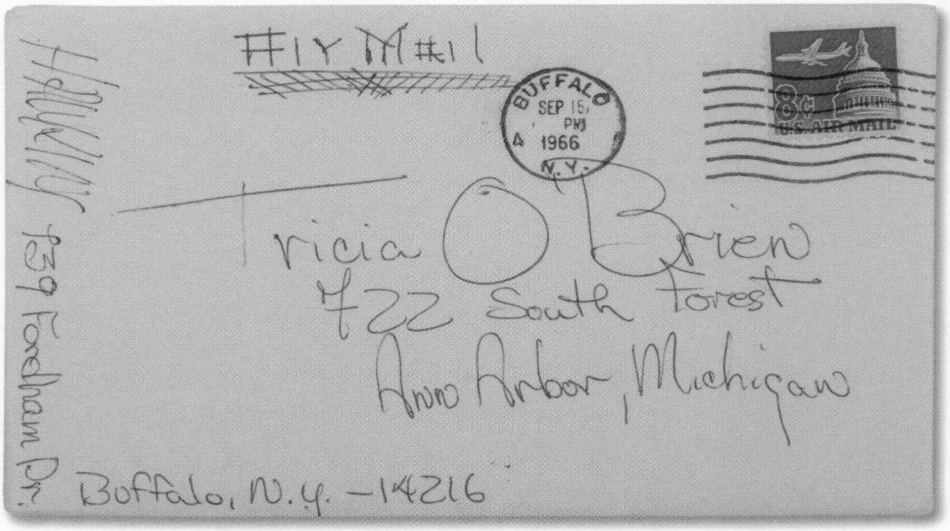
BUFFALO
SEP 15
PM
4 1966
N.Y.
8¢
U.S. AIR MAIL
Tricia O'Brien
722 South Forest
Ann Arbor, Michigan
139 Fordham Dr.
Buffalo, N.Y. -14216

My father was a lover of things,
decorative things.

Objects and ornaments, furniture and framed art. Everything from pillows to plant stands, shelves to settees. He loved fabric and lace and thread and yarn. It almost didn't matter what the things were; if they were designed and intended to decorate and furnish a home, if he could see a way for them to decorate a home, if they were beautiful—if he understood them to be beautiful, knew them to be beautiful, saw them as beautiful—whether he owned them or not, he'd notice, pay attention, offer his regard, his respect, his attention, his time.

This doesn't mean he was faithful in his protection of objects, that he saved them on purpose, sheltered them from harm, or ever thought much about who would receive his most prized possessions. When he moved out of my house (after having moved in because we all believed he was dying), out of the home I owned (with my then partner) for ten years, he left behind a few objects that I know he valued, ones associated with personal stories, connected to his past: a gold-handled cane once owned by a great-aunt and a stained glass window that hung in a church in which my grandfather once (and I actually mean once) preached. He didn't bother removing certain pieces of art from the wall—a map of Detroit, a framed ivory necklace, a painting of a male torso in suit and tie—and now these pieces, ones I've grown to love, hang on the wall where I live.

But otherwise, and what seems strange for a man who loved things so, he resisted bequeathing them directly to any individual as he was actively dying. For all of the conversations my brother and I listened to regarding his plans

love

to take his own life should treatment and pain become unbearable (a move he'd never make), he rarely discussed his belongings, never asked us what it is we'd like, what we wanted, what memento of his existence we'd like to have. Once, I remember him saying, "Your brother gets the art and you get the books," and I was so angry about the reinstitution of his idea of who we were and what we might want that I let the phrase evaporate the same as I did so many of his declarations.

As my father resisted moving from his apartment to the nursing home, with all of the hospice workers, my mother and brother there to support him, to help him figure out what he'd leave to whom, he would only say that the contents of the kitchen would go to Constance and Mikhaila, the two eldest of the grandchildren, and Charles, his grandson, would get the French chair. The rest of it, it seemed, he couldn't care less about, though there wasn't much left, following a number of robberies and the opportunistic gleaning by a few of his "friends," to disperse. But he would not say more than that, and so two weeks later, after he was dead, all decisions regarding the contents of his apartment were left to me.

What of the apparent incongruity between his love for objects and his refusal to ensure their future and care? Lack of preparation? Perhaps. Denial regarding his own mortality? Most certainly. But there was more to it than that. The thing that my father loved about each object, I began to realize, had more to do with its "thingness" than the thing itself.

I'm tired and my mind is
stopping _____ before I
nap it _____ I love you,
So very much ° ° ° ° ° ° ° °

It always happened suddenly, outings with my father. Like he just then, at that moment, got the idea. *C'mon*, he'd say, and no matter what my brother and I were doing—not that we could or would be doing all that much on a Saturday or Sunday when I was five or six or seven—we had to stop, at that very moment, and get in the car. These outings were nothing like the trips we took with Mom, rides to school, to the grocery store, to Pop-Pop's work or house. With her, driving was a part of rhythm and predictability. It had a purpose that made sense not only to us, but within a frame for the rest of the world as well. With my father, both the driving and the car were afterthoughts, nearly insignificant except for the fact that on foot we could have never done what we were going to do.

What we were usually going to do was procure something—usually cigarettes from 7-Eleven. Sometimes there'd be enough money for me and my brother to each get our own Slurpee, sometimes we had to share one, sometimes we could each get a penny pretzel rod. More than once I saw him lifting seat cushions in the family room, scavenging for coins before the trip. These times he would make us wait in the car and run in, barefoot and shirtless, prepared to yell at what I can now only assume to be a sixteen- or seventeen-year-old cashier about the ridiculous 7-Eleven dress code. Sometimes he had to scream. Sometimes he didn't. Only once did he return without the cigarettes. On this day he encountered the owner of the store, a large mustachioed man who wasn't going to have been afraid of my skinny, shaggy-haired father wearing nothing but cutoffs. The owner understood. A man without shoes and a shirt would likely not have his license with him either, and I like to think that my father, in that moment, became the only person ever carded for buying tobacco at a 7-Eleven in the mid-1970s. Through two layers of glass— the windshield and 7-Eleven's clear front wall—I watched as my father became so angry he no longer appeared human, becoming, before my eyes, a super-short stop-motion animation drawn in soft graphite or charcoal, all blurry and fierce, jaw thrust out, arms waving overhead, swears flying from his gaping mouth spelled with all the nonalphabetic symbols I knew: !#$&*%!

What I always wished we were going to do, even though we only did this a couple times, was "collect" fieldstones. Twice I remember this adventure with him, my father pulling into a future subdivision, tires spitting dust clouds in the midsummer heat as he drove toward a large pile of stones that had been pulled from the earth removed from digging large holes that would one day become basements.

Both of these collecting adventures happened when I was only three or four, in construction sites of soon-to-be curved-road subdivisions in Sterling Heights, Michigan, the same place my parents bought their first home, the one we lived in before we moved to Grosse Pointe, a newly built ranch in a newly minted city, one of the second-wave white flight communities in the Detroit area. They happened in a Ford Pinto, the very car made famous by the personal injury case *Grimshaw v. Ford Motor Company*, the one involving a death following a rear-ending accident and a verdict that awarded the plaintiffs well over one hundred million dollars in damages.

Waiting a half beat after he exited the car, I used both legs to press open the passenger door before stepping out onto the camel-colored dirt, my Keds quickly moving into step a few paces behind him. It didn't take long to realize my father seemed to have forgotten I was there. I shot around him to the right and quickly scrambled up to the top of a ten-foot pile of stones, a vantage point from which I could look out over the razed emptiness, note a gargantuan lone willow arched out across the banks of a teeny tiny brook.

Cars whizzed by on some distant-mile road as my father studied the pile. He didn't want any old stones. He was looking for the most interesting, the prettiest. Ones that were nearly spherical, having been tumbled by the glaciers thousands of years before, deposited on the surface of the earth. He began moving them, most of which took him two hands to pick up and relocate. What he didn't want he'd fling a bit to the left with a dull *cru-thunk*. What he did want he would more delicately place on the right. He was in a kind of trance, an intense space of focus he entered for nearly half an hour. When he had about twenty-five or so rocks in the to-go pile, he seemed to suddenly remember I was with him. He looked up, snapped his fingers, and pointed to me, then the ground next to him.

Ten seconds later, I was by his side. He nodded toward a pile of smaller rocks, ones he could one-hand with no problem. *Get those*, he commanded. Together we loaded his selections into the back of the subcompact, he lifting the larger pieces, me hefting the smaller stones. When the tailpipe was nearly hitting the ground, *That's enough. Get in.*

The rocks became a part of an embankment around a section of garden on the front lawn of our house, a garden in which he planted a wide range of bulb flowers, roses, and a fruitless olive, a tree with two-inch thorns, making it impossible to climb. It was a garden he was nearly always working in. Watching him there, I came to understand the nature of his desire as connected always-only to his own projects, creations lush and full in color, solicitous of meaningful line. It took me years to realize that in all of this energy, excitement, and generosity toward gardens, flowers, art, and making, he never left much room for other people. It took a tremendous amount of space, apparently, for considered and considerate design.

I don't care so much for material things, physical decorative objects. I sometimes have to curtail the deep desire to divest myself of nearly all of my belongings. Nearly all my belongings. As I imagine what it would look like to pare down to furnishings enough for a one-bedroom, perhaps even a studio, apartment, I realize I would need to think about the boxes of saved paper: old photos, grade school and high school writings and awards, papers from college and graduate school. And letters. What would I, could I, do with the letters?

It's not as though I have all the letters ever written to me. I know for a fact that I do not. Over a lifetime I have developed a way of deciding which cards and letters are keepers and which ones go. I don't hold onto letters to create a historical record of my communications or to document my relationships. Though I save letters that we might most broadly define as love letters, sentimentality and nostalgia are not central to the decision-making process. The myth of romantic love, heteronormative desire, and our cultural obsession with "happily

ever after" have nothing to do with my letter-saving practices. I do not save letters because they offer me a way of understanding, reframing, or making sense of my past.

The letters I save are those in which I am most able to make and remake my own future connections with and to desire. Desire for another, often. Desire for writing: always. Desire that for me expresses and originates in a bodily understanding of queerness; my own sensational and affective understanding of being queer.

"Queerness," José Esteban Muñoz explains, "is a structuring and educated mode of desiring that allows us to see and feel beyond the quagmire of the present." The love letter offers us a space for desiring beyond whatever mundane, difficult, painful realities we may be experiencing in the present. Not every love letter written offers the same potentiality of queerness, but the love letter itself is a form that always provides an aperture to the queer.

Through the letter, writers are offered an opportunity to reinvent and reimagine themselves in and through and for the eyes of another. We are ourselves, writing for another. We can become someone different, or no one at all. The letter-as-object sent forward in space and time comes into the hands of another person and is translated through reading into their own reality in this future-now time. If saved, the letter opens us well beyond the two-point relationality of an initial-writing-now that becomes a later-reading-then.

In every letter written in and with and toward a space for transformative possibility, there is the opening for infinite potential worlds and realities. Every time I read a letter I have saved, I find myself that much better able to understand the potential in Maurice Merleau-Ponty's notion of transposition, a concept, Gayle Salamon explains, that "describes the process by which the desire that houses itself becomes my body itself—not held proximately by thought, but felt and experienced (as opposed to only referred to) through and as the body."

I desire to write the letter.

I desire to read the letter.

I desire to save the letter.

I desire to read the letter again.

I reach for the letter with my hand because of a desire to experience the hand of another.

I read, and the body of the letter enters and becomes a part of my own body.

Words written in a space of desire always provide me an aperture for my own queer bliss.

love

By the time I was twelve, I was aware that my father was emotionally disconnected. Often personable, regularly entertaining, he used a well-scripted show of exuberance and panache to simulate engagement with other adults and even with my friends. With anyone else around other than me, my mother, and/or my brother, my father surged with energy and connected with others through humor. If there were no other observers, no audience, he was often chronically distant, desperately withdrawn. I wanted the attention that he had for others, and I asked him to spend time with me. Just me. Alone. *We could do something together,* I offered. *Maybe,* I suggested, trying to choose something that would appeal to him, *we could go to the art museum. Maybe,* he said, but I knew that he really meant no.

I complained to my mother, telling her that I wanted—that I needed—to spend time with Dad by myself, to do something with him. She must have been puzzled, I imagine, by his reticence, and I wonder whether she had to cajole and guilt him into it or whether he simply took the suggestion in the same manner he executed most tasks of his suburban life: with the resolve of a labor camp prisoner, just another thing he needed to do to survive.

He didn't do this very well, this particular museum visit. I recall it now as lonely, as empty as the floor space in most of the galleries at the Detroit Institute of Arts. Bits and pieces of memory echo like footsteps on the parquet floor. We roamed the galleries together, chatting a little bit, but never really landing on any conversation, never moving into intimate space. I spent the afternoon watching him look, studying him move in close to the pictures, to the paintings, to "see." Whatever he knew about art, whatever information he had that he might have taught me, did not come out of his mouth that day, but I learned a lot. I watched him get scolded by more than one guard when he instinctively raised his hand to touch the dried oil, to feel the brush strokes with his fingertips. *Oh, it's OK,* he'd say in response to their concern. *No, sir,* the guard always replied. *You may not touch the paintings.* My father would roll his eyes and relent at least until the guard was once again out of view. *Would you look at that layering,* he'd say. With no training and no real interest in art, no way of entering his one-sided musings, I had no reply. In those moments, I witnessed the connection I longed for, the intimacy and love that was, I believed, withheld from me. Here, I noted that his love was for craft, for the execution and creation of these works. Here, I started to develop a kind of hate for anything that he loved, out of spite, I suppose, because it had to be that it was that other thing—art, a dog, a garden, design—that was actually in the way of loving me.

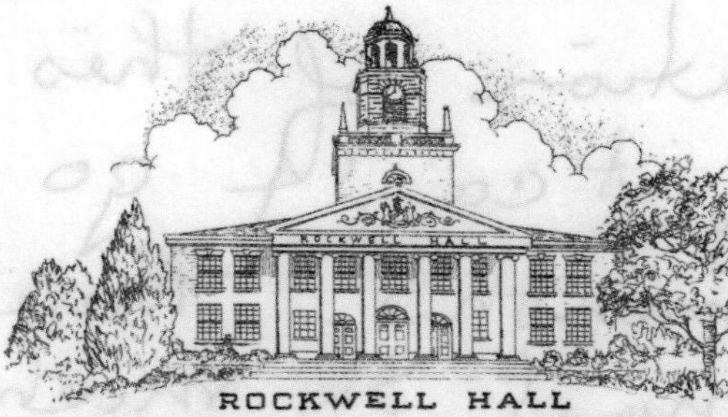

ROCKWELL HALL
State University College
BUFFALO, NEW YORK 14222

Wed. Nite —

Tricia love —

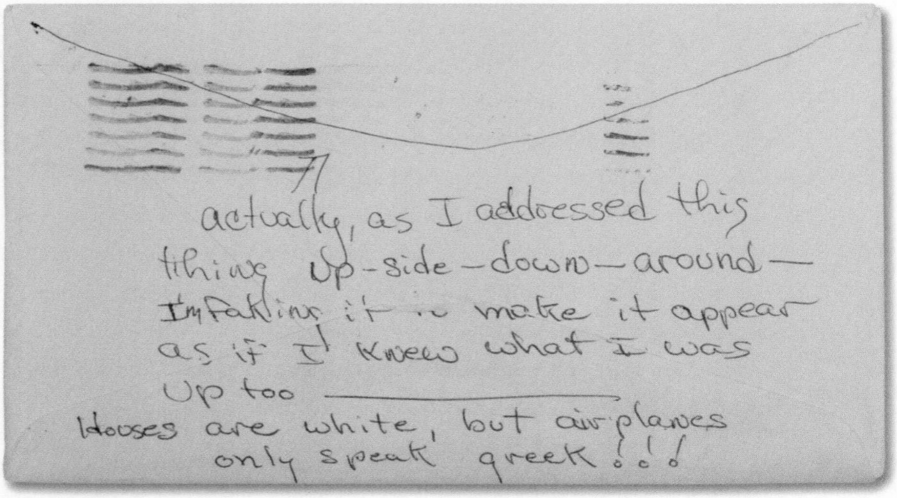
actually, as I addressed this
thing up-side-down-around—
I'm faking it to make it appear
as if I knew what I was
up too
Houses are white, but airplanes
only speak greek!!!

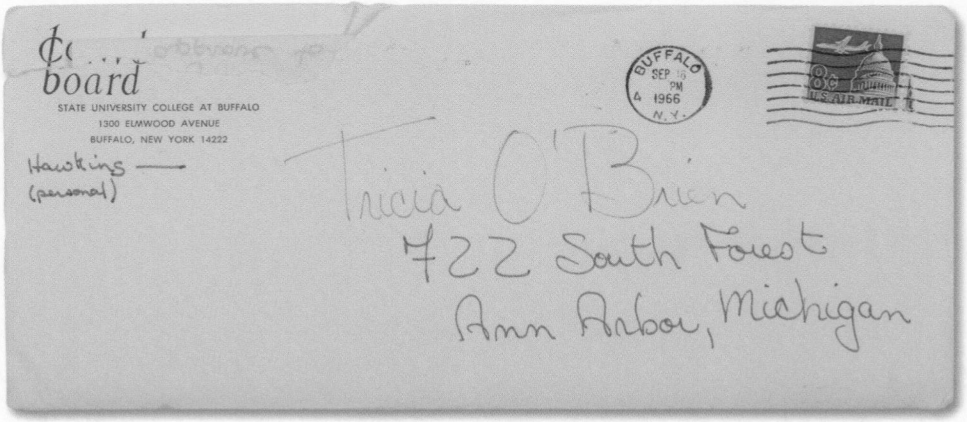
board
STATE UNIVERSITY COLLEGE AT BUFFALO
1300 ELMWOOD AVENUE
BUFFALO, NEW YORK 14222
Hawkins —
(personal)
BUFFALO
SEP 16
PM
4
1966
N.Y.
8¢
U.S. AIR MAIL
Tricia O'Brien
722 South Forest
Ann Arbor, Michigan

The sum total expense in terms of
postage for the twenty letters my
father sent to my mother was $1.78.

He opted for airmail, which required three cents more than the standard cost of ground transportation. On the first six letters, he placed two five-cent stamps, more than enough postage, with the exception of Letter #5, which, it appears, arrived with six cents postage due. If I sent twenty letters today, all of which are now technically "airmail," it would cost me $9.80. Still a bargain. But the cost of the stamp is only one part of the issue.

I like to think about how economics relates to the ecology of the stamp. When my father sent letters, when my mother received them, letters were very much a part of communicative patterns of the day. Their letter writing placed them in community with their parents and their grandparents, with family members; with Americans of all walks of life. Today, it's less than common for the average person to send a letter. Some electronic form of communication would likely be chosen instead. I do not find this shift depressing; it isn't in and of itself a "bad" thing. As sure as I am that we won't ever return to see letters as a primary mode of communication in our world, neither do I believe they—or the book—are ever going to die. Different isn't bad. Different is different.

Staring at the stack, I picture my father's mail, my mother's letters, moving and existing inside a personal epistle community, sliding along, next to and in relationship with all the other letters written person to person, hand to hand, across space and time. I think about the different experience my letters have as they move mostly among flyers, magazines, and third-class mail. I think about how these

letters have lived in our lives. How I have loved letters;
how I have come to love better through these letters. How
I am able to love because of these letters. How it is these
letters are loved.

love

that maze of people ——— a person among
people is more than rare ——— I had
resigned myself to the fact that they were
non-existant, but you changed all that —
and if I die tomorrow then my life had
at least just begun to acquire some
completeness ——— the greatest thing is
that in all probability I'll be alive and
we'll be able to live in that completeness,

Somewhere near the end of that first month my father lived with us, he came in from outside after having a smoke on the deck and caught me standing in the doorway, staring into his room. I was looking at the space he had created; the multiple quilting, beading, needlepoint projects he had begun.

"What do you need?" "Nothing." "What are you looking at?" "Nothing." But, I knew well, I was not looking at nothing. I was looking at him. I was looking at the him that would never be affected by health, would never waste, shrink, or get thrush. I was looking at that which not only kept him alive but allowed him to root.

Rootedness, his textiles continue to teach me, is ours to both make and discover. It is there for us to both realize and find. We are not without roots, even when it appears that we are; the roots we assume we have may be insufficient to hold us to the ground.

Rootedness, I come to learn, enables a kind of longevity, a semblance of eternal life.

This is the place from which we can and will create great work.

She pushes open the heavy door of the sorority house, relaxing into the slight cool of the entryway's interior. Only the first week of school and she's already sick of classes. Not liking most of them. Wondering now, on a regular basis, if she doesn't want to be a teacher, why she is still here. If you don't want to do what you're in school for, what is the point?

It's still early in the day, before noon, and the sun hasn't yet raised the temperature of the front of the house. By two o'clock, both the living room and the composite room will be uncomfortably warm. By four o'clock, the upstairs will be stifling, so most of the women will gather in the dining room to study after dinner, after dark.

She looks at her watch. Lunch in a few minutes and then skit practice later in the afternoon. She should take this time to study, but she'd rather practice her lines. She's got the lead in the skit they're doing for rush, and she wants to do a good job.

She cuts through the dining room on her way to the backstairs, glancing quickly at her mailbox, hoping, yet not expecting, to see something there. She tells herself there's no reason to look, but she can't help herself. And anyway, it's totally fine if there's nothing. She got a letter just yesterday, on his birthday. And they talked on the phone. And she had written to him. And he would have been busy. There wouldn't be another one yet. It would be, she decides, too soon.

But a sliver of the now-familiar blue-gray color catches her eye. Even before she can think, before she can put into words what she knows, she experiences a thrill, a surge of excruciating glee that presses upward from her diaphragm and pushes hard on the bottom of her heart. Reaching forward, she pulls out the letter and runs her finger across the red ink of her address, turns it to read his location-less return address: *Hawkins—who knows where???*

She stops, notices she's holding her breath, and exhales. Does she open this now or save it for later? No one is around, she decides, no reason to wait.

Sticking the tip of a finger under the back flap of the envelope, she hooks and tears a corner, and then plunges and firmly draws her finger across the top, creating a seam.

She presses lightly on the corners, revealing tiny typed print, some sort of form. She slides the paper out, unfolds it to find that he's mailed a Western Union form. She notes the details. Two check marks in boxes: night-letter, shore-ship. The Wizard of Oz, it appears, will need to pay. Time of day? "Never-Never," which apparently happens on his birthday.

He addresses her as "The Girl I love." An opening she considers. One she desires. Even so. She may be the girl he loves, but is she this girl? The kind who gets this letter? Who knows how to respond to a letter like this?

Standing there, in the back hallway, she reads and rereads what he's written. It's a kind of apology, for what, she's not sure.

He's anxious that she found him cold on the phone, distant and disinterested. Sure, he was quiet. Talking on the phone isn't like it was at camp, talking in the evening, on the steps of her cabin, at the campfire, in between activities, whenever they could. She's been unsure, too. Of what to say. Of what it might mean.

Had he not written her, it's doubtful she'd have written him first. It was fun, the summer they had. But they lived far apart. He in Buffalo, she here in Ann Arbor. She has school, and so does he. Her mother, still sick, and never getting better. It all seemed a kind of barrier for a connection of any permanent kind.

Even more, she wondered, would her father even like him? And his parents, the way he talks about them, was it even possible for them to like her? And why jump to these questions anyway? What does this mean? Does it even have to mean anything at all?

But she's never met anyone like him.

Never gotten letters like these.

Never experienced the freedom she's discovered in the way her heart now feels, the confidence and exhilaration that merely thinking about him can bring.

She has no answers, and so she goes upstairs, pulls out a piece of paper, and opens, *Dear George*. She hears and ignores the buzzer for lunch.

It was on a trip to Washington, DC, that brought my mom and her friend Chris back to Broomall, Pennsylvania, the city in which she lived until she was three. The city was a point of connection between them. It was the site of my mom's first home, and Chris had lived there until she moved to Grosse Pointe, with her husband, as a result of his career. Following a visit with some of Chris's friends, my mom asked whether they might drive by the house in which she was born. She had an address: 32 South Green Hill Road. Chris knew exactly where that was.

An elderly woman was on the walkway in front of the house when they pulled up. My mom noted the woman's surprise, her hesitation, and so she spoke before stepping forward: *Hi! I was born in this house,* she began. The woman resisted the story: *That can't be true. I have lived in this house since it was built.* My mom tried a second time with more detail, starting with her name: *I'm Patricia O'Brien, daughter of Charles and Mildred O'Brien.* The woman brightened, exclaimed, *Oh, my! You're Charlie and Frances's daughter! You lived next door! I'm your Aunt Aileen!* She began to cry. She called to her next-door neighbor, *Look who's here! It's Patsy! It's Charlie and Frances's daughter!* Aileen and Dot invited my mom and Chris into the house for tea.

Huddled around the table in a small kitchen made smaller by all of the knickknacks, my mom listened intently as stories her father had told were confirmed. Turns out, Charlie, my Pop-Pop, had once won the neighbor's house in a poker game. It was also true that he had given the deed back to Dot on the sly, telling her that it was her house now, to sign the deed, put it in a safe-deposit box in the bank, to never let her husband know. Pop-Pop told Aileen: *He's a good man when he doesn't drink, but he's a drunk. The drink will kill him.* Dot reported that Pop-Pop told her that if she ever revealed to her husband that she had the deed to the house, it was all on her.

They were wonderful people, just wonderful! The only reason I own my house is because of your father. He was such a good man.

Then, Aileen told another story, one my mother hadn't heard:

One morning your father went off to work, taking the car with him. Your mother came over and said, Aileen, I have a favor to ask. I need to go down to St. Vincent's Hospital. Today is the day that I get to pick out my baby. Aileen was clearly so proud of having been a part of the event my mother couldn't bring herself to say that though she had always suspected she was adopted, this is, would be, and, in this moment, would become the story of how she finally found out.

I'm Sad
and it's 2:45

Tricia —— I love you
Tried to call you alo
phone had no one to

First, she read to me, but by the time I was two, I was reading to her. My mother and I would sit in a chair, or on the couch; in my bed, on the floor; me perched on her thighs, the book lounging on mine. What began as simple recitation soon shifted to actual decoding, and by the time I was school age we'd move into literary discussion as well.

My literacy narrative, the one my mother tells, has three chapters: The Parking Lot, The Allmachers' House, Kindergarten.

love.

The Parking Lot: "You were maybe eighteen months old. This itty-bitty thing. You already loved television, and I would put you in your swing in front of *Sesame Street*. I could tell you were learning because every time you were really thinking, really concentrating, that binky of yours would move up and down in your mouth a million miles a second. One day we were walking in the parking lot of a mall. Macomb Mall, I think it was. I was holding your hand—you usually insisted on walking, didn't want to be carried, didn't like the stroller—and it sounded to me, at first, like you were randomly calling out letters, in this singsongy voice. R, P, A. Short pause: N, T, L . . . M, B, H. And so on, and I really wasn't paying a ton of attention, and then you stopped dead in your tracks, let out a scream, and just started pointing. AHHHHH. What? What, Amy? I asked. You pointed, furrowed your little brows, and screamed again, and I got down to your eye level to see that you were pointing at a license plate. You had been reading the letters off the license plates. You didn't know the letter Q. Q? Q? I said. Q. You repeated and read the plate, who knows, something like B Q D. You were one and a half, and you could read."

The Allmachers' House: "I was in the kitchen and the phone rang. It was Mrs. Allmacher. You've got to come down here, she said. Why? Is everything all right? She told me yes, everything was fine. But that you were reading the little ticker tape at the bottom of the television or something. Maybe it was the one announcing the coming of a storm, or whatever they used to flash on the TV when they ran that Emergency Broadcast sound. You understood that this was information that the adults might need to know, and since they weren't in the room, you were calling out the information to her from the family room to the kitchen. I told her as nicely as possible I already knew that you could read. Yes, wasn't that amazing. All that. She couldn't get over it. You were three."

Kindergarten: "I got the call. You failed the kindergarten exit exam. I thought, What in the hell? Well, you and I marched right on up there. I had you sit in the waiting room while I took a look at your test, listened to what they had to say. It was the days of paper, so it was easy to see what had happened. It was a bubble test, and you had rushed. Gotten off by a question, so nearly every single one was wrong. But there were enough right, by chance, that the teachers weren't completely convinced. I called you in. You were sitting outside the office up to this point. You came in, and I told Sister Lois she could choose any book off the shelf and open it. She chose one, handed it to me, I handed it to you. Read, I told you. You started mid-sentence at the top of the page. You read a couple sentences and then asked, For how long? That's enough, Sister Lois said. You were told it was important to learn how to take your time. You were told you needed to slow down. You were five. You were promoted to first grade."

I ask my mom when I learned to write. She stops. Thinks a moment. Turns to me and says, "You just did."

love

11 / September 16, 1966

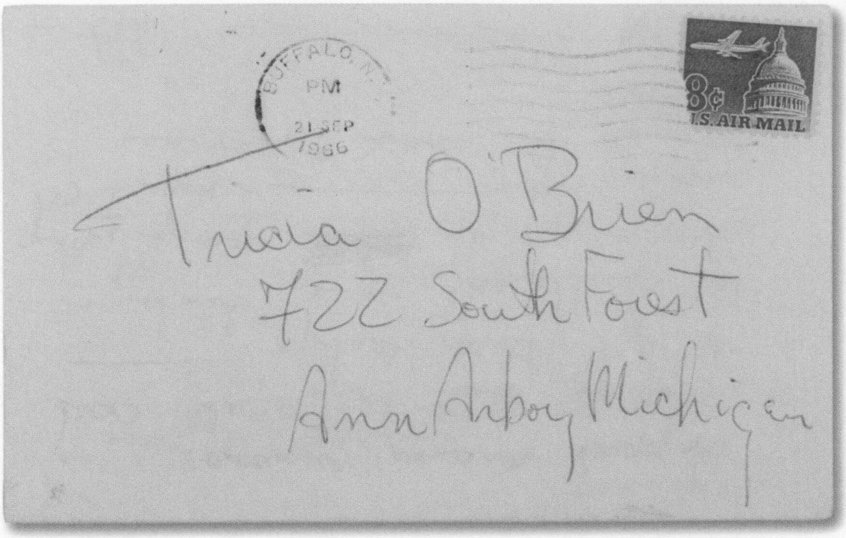
BUFFALO, N.
PM
21 SEP
1966
8¢
U.S. AIR MAIL
Tricia O'Brien
722 South Forest
Ann Arbor Michigan

"I don't exactly regret having you two, but I wouldn't do it again."

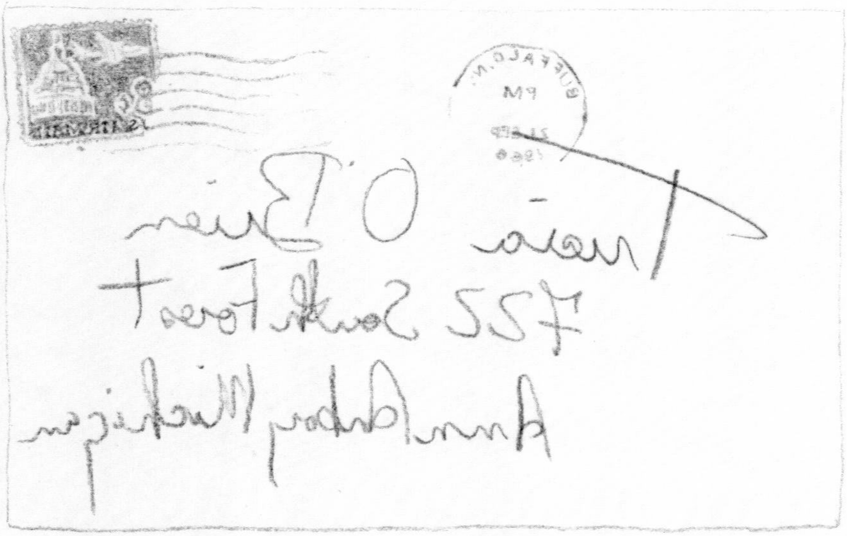

I don't recall where or when my father said these words; I think I was twenty-four. What I know for sure is these are the very words he said, in their precise order. I know this for certain because of the way the words landed in me, filled me, knew me.

The words entered through my eyes, not my ears. They were words I could see, words that made things clearer, yet more complicated than ever before. They landed softly, gently, just below my cerebellum, on my brain stem, and washed down the back of my neck, a slender single sentence as warm sensate stream. Pooling along my spine, in the space between my scapula, they rested for a moment before popping forward, pitched toward the sternum, pushing open an unknown-to-me backdoor in my heart.

Around and around I pumped those words, breaking them apart under pressure of ventricles, in the swoosh of blood through each chamber into individual letters, no longer readable as language, present only as sign. Life currents unmaking these characters, opening them into lines, into strands, recognized now, in my body, as genetic code. As the words traveled through my arteries, my veins, I experienced a steady, deep, reflexive wash of calm. What once were words, comprehended by my mind, were now, in my corpus, experienced as phenomenological knowledge, autonomic understanding. Exactly what it was I understood, I could not yet say.

Love

In the first few years following my parents' divorce, meals in public space were the setting for most any exchange between my father and me. Red cracked vinyl seats, liquid yellow fake butter topping on white toast, and waitresses with smoking habits served to reinforce a father-daughter relationship that depended upon a thermos full of Bunn-O-Matic coffee for its intimacy. My father and I were "the same," I thought, as had been illustrated to me through hours and hours of conversation, creative exchange, and idea production. We had, I believed, made a wordless pact to remain connected not by what was made explicit but by ideas existing just out of reach of language itself. We enjoyed each other's company, playing around with and in words this way.

It was up north, in the Port Hope Bar, over $1.50 hamburgers and 35¢ shells of Budweiser, no more than two feet from a pool table surrounded by men in full beards, mesh-backed baseball hats with heavy equipment insignia, that Dad announced that he was gay. I wasn't surprised by the announcement. I was betrayed by the delivery, by his selection of the location, by his clear disregard for what I believed had been a tacit agreement in our post-divorce life: we limit our conversation to public spaces because public spaces limit personal conversation.

I heard what he said, but I suddenly became deaf. Blood pulsed behind my eyes and in my ears. Dad's lips moved, but I could hear nothing but the thumping of my own circulatory system. He was telling me something about how hard this was, about how he had such a difficult time with it all. But, I could hear none of it.

Goddamn you, Dad, I thought. *This coming-out moment. This moment to name. It was supposed to have been mine.*

Though I was not at all surprised by the content of his announcement in the Port Hope Bar, the news he delivered on a summer Sunday morning at Harry's on Mack Avenue shocked me. As if on cue, at almost the exact second my poached eggs and pancakes and his eggs and toast were laid on the table, he looked down and told me he had some bad news. Just as he had imagined, just as he had suspected, he was HIV+.

"What the fuck, Dad," I said.

He never looked up. His left hand fiddled with the fork on the napkin. I was relieved that there were no threatening figures only inches from us, no farmers with guns. But I was also annoyed that he had chosen to tell me sitting in the familiar normalcy of this family restaurant booth.

"What the fuck were you thinking? It's 1995 for Chrissakes. You know how people get HIV. What were you doing?"

His hands shook, and I could see slender tears on his cheeks, but I was not moved. I did not relent.

"Dad!" I whisper-shouted when he didn't respond. "I demand you tell me now. I want to know exactly how you got this."

His answer came so easily, so quickly. The words and story were so tight. I knew immediately it was bullshit. But, I accepted it because there was nothing else to do. Because I had asked for it. Because cultural narratives regarding HIV make it seem as though knowing where and how and who may have been involved in any particular infection are our business. The details of one person's story relevant to all, logic created via the rhetoric of "safety" and "public health."

But honesty isn't necessarily located in fact. Truth isn't something to be exacted on demand. And words, spoken or written, are never able to take what isn't and make it so.

When I was in the eighth grade, I fell in love for the first time. Her last name started with a C, mine with an H. Since we were seated in alphabetical order, her desk was second or third in the first row, and mine in the second row, a couple more behind hers. From here, this perfect position, I had my first sustained experience in learning how, without being noticed, to watch.

She'd come into the class, as most girls would, binder pressed to her chest, a final coat of armor atop the already nearly impermeable layers of clothes—turtleneck, Oxford button-down, sweater—that left everything about her body to the imagination. She and the other popular girls, all femme-presenting in hot-rollered ribbon-weave barretted hair, sporting makeup in every possible shade of pink, would whisper and giggle at the front of the room before sliding confidently and easily, just as the bell rang, into their seats. It wasn't a conscious move for me, but I wore my binder slung low like the boys, who, if they had one at all, carried them down at their sides, slotted across their right or left hands held in the shape of a C, a weapon ready to be wielded if necessary, with an easy open-arm swing. I took my seat as they did: immediately. Likely for the same reason: to watch the girls as they found theirs.

All of my friends were girls, and yet I found it paralyzing to speak with her. So, I wrote her notes. About what, I cannot recall. I do know that I wrote to her differently than I wrote to my other friends. I wrote nothing about other people in our class. I wrote with intensity and conviction. I wrote because it felt good. I wrote for myself. I wrote only for her.

I started slowly, in October, perhaps dropping one or two notes a week. She didn't often— perhaps even ever—write back. But she would always, after reading a carefully placed, meticulously folded letter, turn around and smile. If she had asked me to, I know I would have stopped. But with her acknowledgment as encouragement, I increased my productivity, covertly delivering sometimes as many as four notes a week. It was a private game.

A secret exchange. I had gotten her attention, and it felt good to have her respond, it felt good to believe I was bringing her joy.

With this opportunity for sustained attention, I moved from the simple act of watching to learning how to notice: What she wore. When she was sick. Where she looked. Whom she watched. How she held her pencil. How she tucked her feet inside the metal basket under the desk. What made her laugh. How green her eyes were. How she always smiled wide, laughed with an open mouth. How her teeth appeared straight beneath braces that would soon be coming off.

One day in December, before class, she slid into the seat directly in front of me and wheeled around, placing on my desk a single turquoise Barbie shoe. Later that day, or maybe that week, I found out she was leaving. Moving to Minneapolis, I think it was. Somewhere far. Somewhere I knew nothing about. What I did know: I would likely never see her again. And, I never did.

I didn't see then, but cannot ignore now, the symbolic connection between the shoe and the story of Cinderella. More than thirty years later, with this narrative as frame, I fantasize about her, somewhere out there. She's queer. She's femme. She's still beautiful and smart and funny and kind. She's available. She'd find me attractive. If only I still had the shoe. If I still had the shoe, I would go looking for her. Me, now, as this dandy, this transgenre prince, I would place it back on her foot, or in this case, back into her hand. Return her possession as an opening to rewrite our connection.

But I do not have the shoe. It, like the notes I wrote, is long gone.

Yet the memory of the shoe remains always with me. I often thank her for this gift, an image by which I can return to trace my journey toward writer, creator; a sexually desiring, and desirable, producer of words.

To date, I've identified seven reasons I love letters, all of which can be understood in terms of the ways they, as a literary genre, provide a writer endless potential in terms of content, one accessed because of the form.

1. A letter foregrounds the notion of dialogue. I record, form, my ideas for you; you return with a response for me. Whether responded to or not, the form itself is written with the intention and hope, with the conviction in the relevance, of communicative exchange.

2. A letter establishes a spatial relationship with respect to writing and reading: I wrote this here, you will read it over there. Letters participate in physical, literal literacy circulation and offer us many lessons on what it means for an idea to be in motion.

3. The letter draws attention to the writer/reader relationship, the idea that one person has written and made an idea, created a reality on the page. Then another person, as intended reader, will decode and unmake the meaning as it had been originally inscribed. A letter sent always anticipates the mirrored response of another. A letter back allows us to look again at ourselves as a literary reflection.

4. Each letter stands as a space of endless possibility for the expression of self—any self they already recognize, intend, or seek to imagine. The private space of the personal letter enables us to identify and reinvent ourselves; let it all out on the page. In a letter we create ourselves with and as and because of another; we are able to manifest an identity with and as and in spite of a self.

5. Letters may contain multiple modes of writing, juxtapose a wide range of genres and styles. They may, and often do, make sudden and numerous shifts in tone, and still they are able to be read

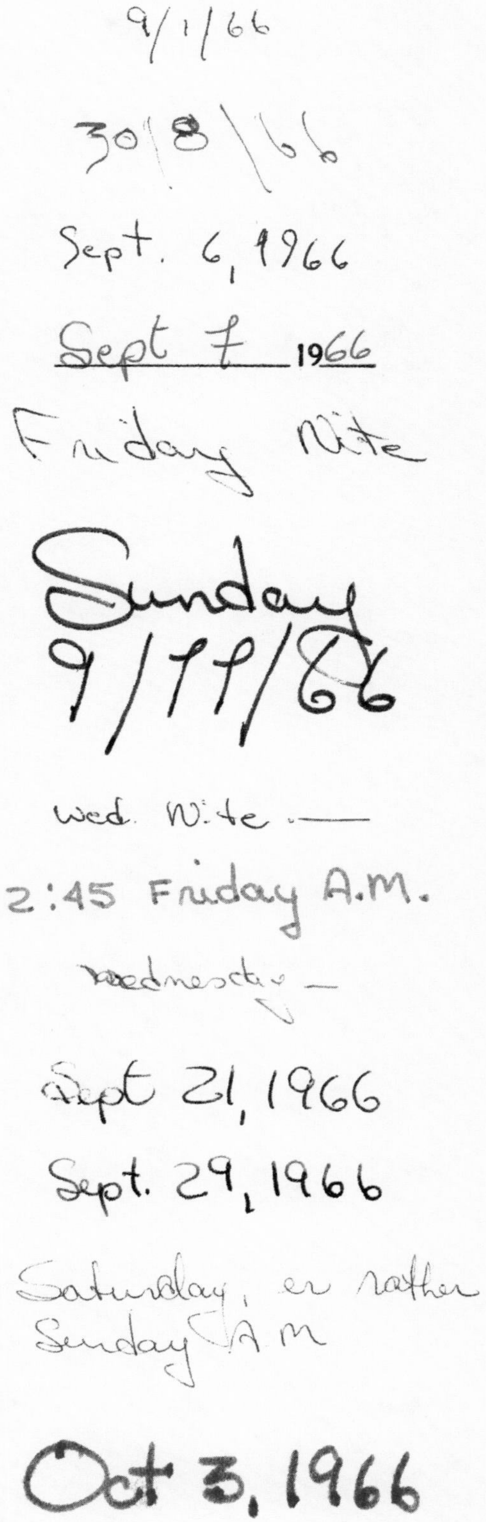
9/1/66
30/8/66
Sept. 6, 1966
Sept 7 1966
Friday Nite
Sunday
9/11/66
Wed. Nite —
2:45 Friday A.M.
Wednesday —
Sept 21, 1966
Sept. 29, 1966
Saturday, or rather
Sunday A.M
Oct 3, 1966

and understood. We can try things out in a letter: new ideas, new words, new constructions.

6. An exchange of letters between two people, in any particular moment, is always connected to an ancestry of letter writing and establishes for those writing the potential of becoming connected to both a literary legacy and a future filled with words.

7. On the page, in the body of the letter, we can offer to another a present, or prescient; secret, or sacred, version of ourselves. Through letters, from our hands to theirs, theirs to ours, we present words as ourselves, we accept their words as them. Here we may find our ways to becoming a different self. Written first by us, read by another, recognized in the exchange as legitimate, as a possible latent or future self.

...what happened afte...

called parents

a. Dad doesn't quite believe we're _not_ married

b. Mums guessed we wer...

c. Steve thinks we're nut...

~~the Guys~~

well they wanted to kn... something 'cause they'd barely talk to me when I got back. Lucia sai... ...ave to tell ~~you~~ on he... ...was much better that...

What I remember about the moment he told me of his seropositive status? Everything. I can see, hear, and feel it all. That scene, like the one in which he tells me he's gay in a bar in Port Hope, Michigan, is hyperreal. In these moments, we are on some theater-of-the-absurd stage. He and I, characters in a play, each of us in our roles. He as longtime, closeted gay man coming out: for two different reasons, in strikingly similar ways. I, as assumed-to-be sympathetic child, with resentment for him, for stories that always seem to overshadow, diminish, and somehow minimize me.

In these scenes, adaptations of scripts outlined by the dominant coming-out narrative, my feelings moved quickly, easily into rage. It was prescriptive, so easy, to inhabit the swelling desire to beat the crap out of something. Comforting and familiar to experience the severing of legs and head from my trunk, energy radiating from my breastbone down my arms to my hands, taking form as fists. I was good in this role as a young prince, upstaged by the queen. Good, we both were, as characters playing parts in the dominant narratives of our culture, foils for conflicts already assumed and understood.

When my father tells me, "I don't exactly regret having you two, but I wouldn't do it again," there is no script. No stage. No roles. No conflict. No response. There is no him versus me, no me versus him. No we. No us. No once. No was. No could have. No will never be.

All there is then, in that moment—an ever-never-now—is universe as art.

As love: Beyond us, as it has always been; not necessarily as it was meant to be.

Love

BUFFALO, N.Y.
PM
21 SEP
1966
1A
will write more
later but I'm
late for my first
class & have to
run!!!!!

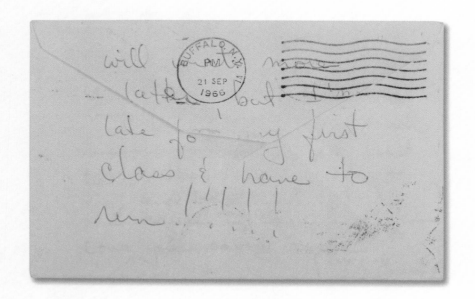

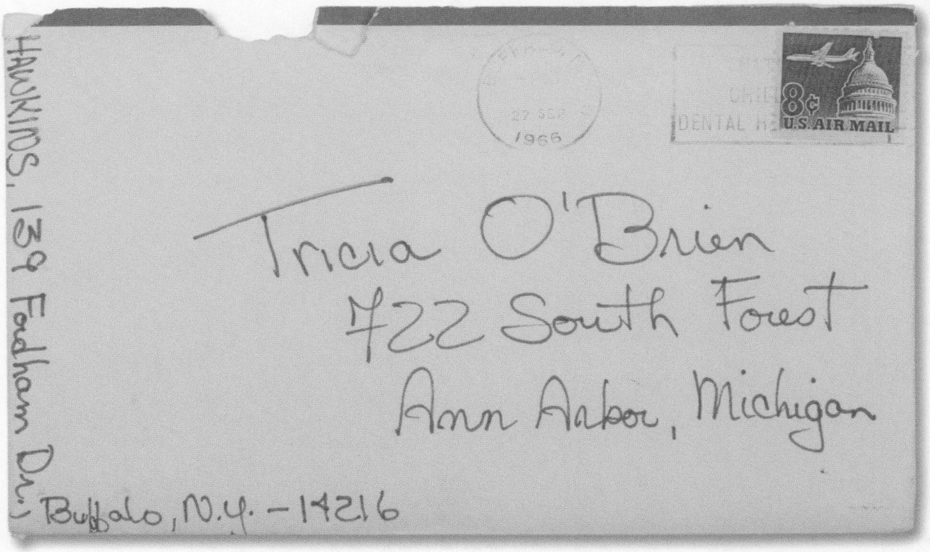
HAWKINS, 139 Fordham Dr.,
Buffalo, N.Y. - 14216
27 SEP
1966
8¢
U.S. AIR MAIL
Tricia O'Brien
722 South Forest
Ann Arbor, Michigan

I love you for all the forevers,

Giorgio

Three full years—almost to the day—go by
before I read the letters a third time. I'm in
Sedona, Arizona, beginning a monthlong
self-created writing retreat. This time, I'm
completely alone.

There's no lover. There are no colleagues. No other writers or friends. I've recently left my partner of nineteen years. I'm starting over: beginning again, it seems, to reread these letters in the same moment all things feel as though they have come to a close.

I had always noticed the affective marks my father makes throughout these letters, hyperbolic dashes that make visible his pausing between thoughts. But now, reading in the shadow of the red rock landscape, it's all I can see. I fixate on them. Do they function only as bridges, connective tissue between gaps? Or are they indicative of the lacerations, faults, and fissures in the narrative he seemed to be working so hard to create?

My father presses pen tip to paper surface and reveals himself between statements. His epistolary synapses make tangible the moments before words land, the ethereal space of imagining and desire, the interplay between what is and isn't there. Physically engaging with the letters, his hand and arm help him decide what he next wants to say. And so, I quit reading and start listening. I stop looking at the letters only as texts and consider their auditory artistry, the composition as visual design.

I open the first letter sitting on a couch in a place where the surface of the earth appears stained with blood. By the final letter, I am once again sitting in the kitchen on the fake brick linoleum floor. Listening as he reads to me words that tangle, made stronger not because they're woven in linear order but because they're pressed together in spaces of desire that never touch.

Here, in these letters, I have never and always existed. Because he wrote them, I live both within and beyond my body. Because she handed them to me, I love both within and without his breath.

I had always known that my parents married young, but it never occurred to me before reading the letters that everything also happened incredibly fast. Their courtship began in the middle of the summer of 1966, continued through a series of letters that began on August 30 and ended on October 2. In the first twelve letters, my parents are not married. In the last eight, they are.

Based upon a couple of conversations with my mother, I fully understand why and how what was going to be a June wedding turned into a September 25 elopement. Her mother was dying; she didn't want to become a teacher. Her father had, at the moment of announcement, booked the Pontchartrain Hotel in Downtown Detroit. A confluence of events prompted her to see this moment as an opportunity to make a decision, to take charge of her own life rather than have decisions be made for her.

I am also fairly confident why my father, a newly (re)closeted gay man, would have wanted to seize upon this moment so intensely, as a way to reinforce whatever story he was telling himself, post-deprogramming, about his own sexuality. He's not gay, he's married. That is the end of that.

Because their decision made possible the occasion for my life, I am not exactly interested in interrogating the speed of these events. I am far more interested in the way the letters call attention to space, initially sent from the Beatles' "Nowhereland," Peter Pan's "Never-never" and "Neverland," and then, in Letter #13, from an equally mythical place he identifies as "definitely our world." Is this a world they shared, the world of lovers? It is, I believe, related, connected, and yet something different, something else.

I inventory, count, and somehow strive to measure a range of elements and aspects of these letters in the hope that I might better understand what happened, map my existence in time and space. Can I, through these scholarly practices, turn this random moment into an inevitability via destiny?

In *A Lover's Discourse: Fragments*, Roland Barthes offers the reader eighty different fragments—words or phrases he refers to as figures—to explore the complicated and complex experiences connected with and to a culturally bound, Western-centric understanding of falling/being/in/out of love. A figure is a word/phrase that is to be "understood, not in its rhetorical sense, but rather in its gymnastic or choreographic acceptation." The figure is constantly moving between the work done by language and the experience-as-concept connected to phenomenological knowing of the body. Barthes explains:

> Figures take shape insofar as we can recognize, in passing discourse, something that has been read, heard, felt. The figure is outlined (like a sign) and memorable (like an image or a tale). A figure is established if at least someone can say: That's so true I recognize that scene of language.

The figure is an impulse, a trace; connective logic, description, grasp for meaning that finds its work to be the articulation of sentences often used to justify cultural belief: why I love this person over that one; why they do/do not love me; why I am/am not lovable; how/why we do/don't need to be in love(d).

Economically, Barthes states: "The figure is the lover at work."

Throughout the twenty letters, my father's writings provide examples of a range of Barthes's figures. Among others, he describes difficulty in writing about love (Inexpressible Love), the importance of affirming through letters and declaration the relevance of love (The Intractable), a lack of ability to explain what's happening even as he believes in the love (Atopos), and the stressful double-edged sword of his own declaration that "night is my favorite time of night" ("And the night illuminated the night"). Most clearly and notably, he repeatedly reaches for the figure of declaration, the avowal of "I love you."

love

In these twenty letters, my father declares his love for my mother forty-nine times. Usually, the statement is direct, a simple writing of those three words at the beginning, middle, or end of a paragraph. Sometimes he varies his style, occasionally writing these words in a larger font, occasionally in Italian, and once in puffy outline letters. Usually, they are a part of a closing, a signing off with "All my love" presented to the reader for the taking. I can understand and see all of the forty-nine I-love-yous connected with and to the power of the phrase as a call for/as/and action. The phrase, even when written down, is a way of speaking aloud, Barthes tells us, "so that you may answer, and the scrupulous form (the letter) of the answer will assume an effective value in the manner of a formula."

I counted twice, wishing for the symmetry and relief of an even fifty I-love-you statements. My desire for that round, full, satisfying number feels like a way to resolve the asymptotic reality of this figure. It seems to me we all wish to make as small as possible the space, pause, gap, anticipation, hope for an equally genuine, clear, direct "I love you" in return.

But the anticipatory character of forty-nine I-love-yous is somehow reinforced by the 449 lines he draws between phrases and thoughts, his own improvised punctuation that seems to denote an ever-never presence-absence of meaning. They make clear a lack in terms of clearly communicated ideas, even as they elucidate the ephemeral presence of space-between-thought. The lines are at once both an absence of language and language-in-the-making; they show us the passage of time in his thinking as a not knowing what else-yet to say even as they welcome the next articulated thought. My father's marks are afigural, in a Barthesian sense. Empty, yet not without meaning. They are a presence of nothingness, similar to the mathematical notation for empty set: {}.

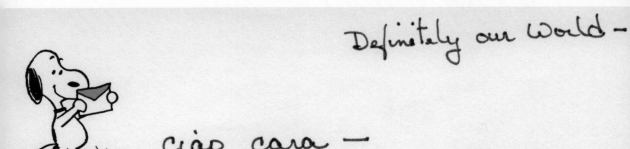

Definitely our world —

ciao cara —

as it is now after supper and

The situation that brought Radclyffe (John) Hall to a love letter–writing relationship that ended up lasting for the rest of her life was one of simple chance. In 1934, John was riding a wave of literary fame, one largely a result of the success of *The Well of Loneliness* (1928), her fifth novel, one that had, by this time, been both banned in England and translated into many languages. She had, by this time, been in a relationship with Una Trowbridge for nineteen years. Pain and weakness in John's right leg, caused by a thirty-year-old riding accident, prompted Una to insist that they travel from their home in England to a spa in Normandy where John had, years before, received some relief. While there, Una suffered a bout of gastroenteritis, and so John sent to Paris for a private nurse. The nurse was twenty-one-year-old Evguenia Souline.

In *Your John: The Love Letters of Radclyffe Hall*, Joanne Glasgow reprints in their entirety 128 of the 576 letters written by Radclyffe Hall to Evguenia Souline between 1934 and 1942. Early in their correspondence, on July 27, 1934, John declares for the first time, "But I love you, I love you." In this same missive, John laments that she is "haunted by the thought of your loneliness, that I am leaving you alone, by my terror that you may fret and get ill, or perhaps do something reckless and most foolish, for to me you seem even younger than your age, and then you have no one to whom you can talk or go to for advice." Whether or not Souline was this desperate, this lonely, this despondent, is impossible to know. We do know that Souline was young, a displaced immigrant from Russia, likely the child of an officer in the White Russian Army. Her training as a nurse, provided by the Red Cross upon her arrival in Paris, would have been convenient; we've no idea whether it was training she desired.

The desperation in John's tone, the near begging for letters in response, often makes me cringe. One can open this volume and skim almost any letter and find some sort of plea for response, for a return of words, a recognition of the self that John presents to her on the page. John wants to be seen, to be loved in return.

My interest in the letters from John to Evguenia has to do with the way it appears John got caught up in the sensation, in the ritual, of using her words for Evguenia instead of using her words for that next book, for her art. I look to the letters from John to Evguenia as confirmation of a conundrum I've experienced in my life: Words written in love can help inspire new ones; words produced through personal desire can help one to become more creative, to generate original thought, innovative prose. These words—this writing produced in the name of love—can also distract, can cause one to become obsessed with and exhaust creative energy so completely that nothing *new* can be imagined at all.

In my experience, when you write in love, words come in an endless stream. When you write in love, you're not writing for the other person as much as you are writing for yourself, for the sensation that you feel, the pricking of your soul, the pulsing of your veins, the throbbing of your crotch. In this state, you're barely aware that there is another person, a precise individual—a human lover—to whom you write. This is not to say that you are unaware that you write to another, but that your concept of them as separate from you is hampered by your own experience of being in love with them. At some point, there is the danger of shifting from writing in love—writing from the point of possibility and all creation—to begin writing for love, writing in the name of love, in the name of the grand idea that is love, the magnificent, magical, mythical state of existence that will always slip from our grasp the minute we hold on too hard. When you write for love, for either the love of your own words or love unrequited, the one to whom you write transitions from a kind of fantastical phantom, nebulous and naughty, to a static other, a lover for whom you write. Without scope or purpose or repositioning, the words you have, they become lost in that Other, in the empty space of that mythological lover.

That which is ever present in the letters from John is never detectable in those from my father. He never begs or pleads; never sounds desperate. Though he continually writes I love you, explaining throughout why he knows people think him a "freak," to be "crazy," he is not writing in the name of love, for the imagined potential of love, writ large, as love story or love relationship, even though I believe him when he repeatedly says he has absolutely no doubt that marrying my mother will be the best thing he ever does. The love story here, the one that matters most to George/Giorgio, is the relationship with and the desire he has always-only for his own art.

It is the most ordinary of acts, the reading of a letter. But as Kathleen Stewart strives to explain, "ordinary is a shifting assemblage of practices and practical knowledges, a scene of both liveliness and exhaustion, as dream of escape or the simple life." In the ordinary, there is always the possibility of a something, a to-be-will-might-happen(ing), in and of itself mundane, yet through the notion of movement, energetic transmission, the ordinary is always laden with possibility, alchemical potentials, imagination, and dreams. There is also the ordinary act of writing a letter: the affective intention of engaging you as an imagined reader opening a space for transmaterialized magic, a becoming: an unfolding event of desire.

My fascination with my father's extended dashes has to do with the ways this afigural discourse communicates the anticipation of and for an ordinary something. The language-less lines, as nondiscursive symbols, express the presence of an affective sensibility. In these lines we are offered access to sensation governing the way a mind moves, to feelings and emotions connected to the generative action of thought.

As the intensity of the narrative builds around a marriage proposal, wedding, and elopement, so do the presence, number, frequency, and relative lengths of the lines my father makes on the page. He's reaching for something here. Words, we might assume, since he's engaged in the work of writing a letter. But it's also clear that he, like any of us who engage in the writing of a letter—especially a love letter—is trying to access a feeling, the sensation of falling, being, and bathing in love. His letters aren't so much connected to a lover's discourses as they are texts expressing one artist's desire.

He's writing to stay connected with the pleasure he finds in and through the processes of making. And, as Barthes tells us, "what pleasure wants is the site of a loss, the seam, the cut, the deflation, the dissolve which seizes the subject in the midst of bliss."

These lines are visual representations of the distances we might travel when we move from idea to idea. These marks offer us a way to imagine the magical work of translating ideas into language, impulse into action, emotion into art, argument into design. They are simultaneously full and empty. They are renderings of rupture, gaps as glory hole. They are figures as fissures; bridges for bliss.

I am comforted by the dependability of these lines, even as I am made anxious by their erraticism, unpredictability. What might this have to do with a daughter-writer trying to understand her father-artist? Barthes explains:

The bliss of the text is not precarious, it is worse: precocious; it does not come in its own good time, it does not depend upon any ripening. Everything is wrought to a transport at one and the same moment.

This transport is evident in painting, today's painting: as soon as it is understood, the principle of loss becomes ineffective, one must go onto something else. Everything comes about; indeed, in every sense everything comes—at first glance.

This first glance is ordinary. We see a thing and say: *Isn't that something?* In these letters my father sees all kinds of things—leaves, trees, a newspaper clipping, a penny—all of which appear to be ordinary.

But, his lines suggest, this is how everything happens: in a moment so ordinary it becomes extraordinary. This is how a letter written in pleasure, even when it doesn't say much of anything, has the potential to offer any reader the feeling they just read something.

Slide your finger into the seam, these marks direct me, and unfold your desire. Pay attention to what's always-never-not-there, and you'll find for yourself an ordinary ability to transport yourself and others toward bliss.

Love

G.F.
SCHULZ
Just hanging around ——
trying not to look to anxious about getting one of your letters!!!!!
Hi Pat - You wouldn't believe my lesson about the Star-Spangled Banner - Ech!
Love
Tom (Lucia)

13 / September 27, 1966

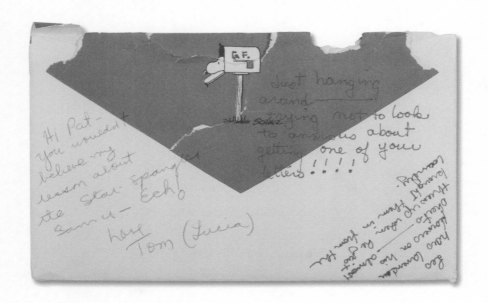

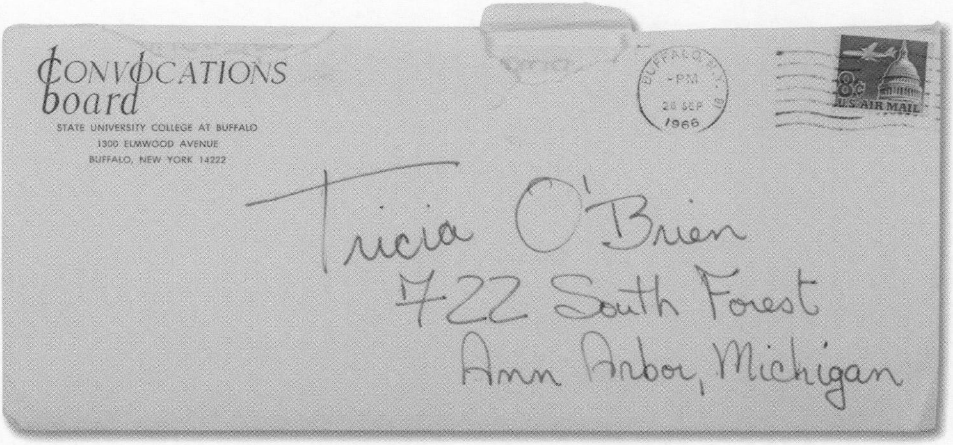
CONVOCATIONS board
STATE UNIVERSITY COLLEGE AT BUFFALO
1300 ELMWOOD AVENUE
BUFFALO, NEW YORK 14222
BUFFALO, N.Y.
PM
28 SEP
1966
8¢
U.S. AIR MAIL
Tricia O'Brien
722 South Forest
Ann Arbor, Michigan

All my love. —————————
Giorgio

My dad once claimed to have had
5,000 sexual partners.

5,000.

Five thousand.

I suppose I could sit and do the math, try to figure out how many years he would have had opportunity to have this much sex. But why? To prove he was lying? More interesting: Why say this at all? Was this his way of claiming connection to a gay life and culture that he had, depending upon your take on the matter, been cheated out of or voluntarily cut himself off from? Was he just trying to be outrageous, over the top, with his statement to get me engaged in some sort of ridiculous fight?

My father graduated from high school in 1962 and, it seems from stories and his own admission, had limited or no homosexual encounters prior to moving to New York City in September of that year when he started school to be a nurse anesthetist. It could be that he was instantly freed from the shackles of his Methodist minister father and entered, from day one, a highly active sex life. He lived and went to school in New York City for the next year and a half or so, but then returned home in the winter of 1964 because he was sick. Mono is what he told me. This is also the illness that somehow evolved into deprogramming— an event I know nothing about, just that it happened—and he convalesced at his parents' house until the fall of 1964, when he enrolled at Buffalo State College because they had a study abroad program in Italy. He completed one year at Buffalo in order to become eligible for the study abroad program and, the next year, joined a fraternity and spent three months in Siena, Italy.

I do not know whether my father had 5,000 partners, but I know that he framed at least 90 percent of his stories, of his history, of his reality, by one of two sentence starters:

Love

"When I was in New York" and "When I lived in Italy." The places themselves are 5,000; they are hyperbole, symbols of the ways that overstatement, exaggeration, and embellishment structured my father's reality.

New York City and, even more, Siena, Italy, were bedrock to my father's identity, but not because he took from these places important relationships and nodal events. These two sites connected him to artistic and queer narratives, to histories and pasts far more colorful and interesting than most of the life he lived. He may have had an active, enjoyable sex life as a gay man in these two places. I very much hope he did. But, he never talked directly about his sexuality in these locations until after he came out, until it became a way of erasing the heterosexual life he had in favor of an alluded-to homosexual life in faraway places, mythological locations by which he could then reinvent a connection to gay culture.

The stories he told never had beginnings, middles, or ends; they involved not one other soul we knew who could corroborate the information. His anecdotes swirled around a sense of body and behavior that emphasized the freedom of youth, of high jinks, and haute couture; romanticism and desire for a physique long gone, one that weighed less than 150 pounds, fit into skin-tight Beatles-style jeans, played jokes on other people, stayed up all night, painted like a madman, smoked and drank coffee or cappuccino as the sun went down, as the sun came up.

These stories were always, I came to understand, about Giorgio, not George. George was the man who worked as an interior designer and lived with us in Grosse Pointe. George was the man who was my father. Giorgio was the artist who lived in New York City and Siena, Italy, and then wrote letters to Tricia.

It strikes me the way narratives are so able to shift and be shifted. To do work you never knew they were doing, never understand they could do.

When George claims 5,000 sexual partners, he unwrites the connection between us.

In Giorgio's Italy, I recognize the ways my life and/as desires intersect with his.

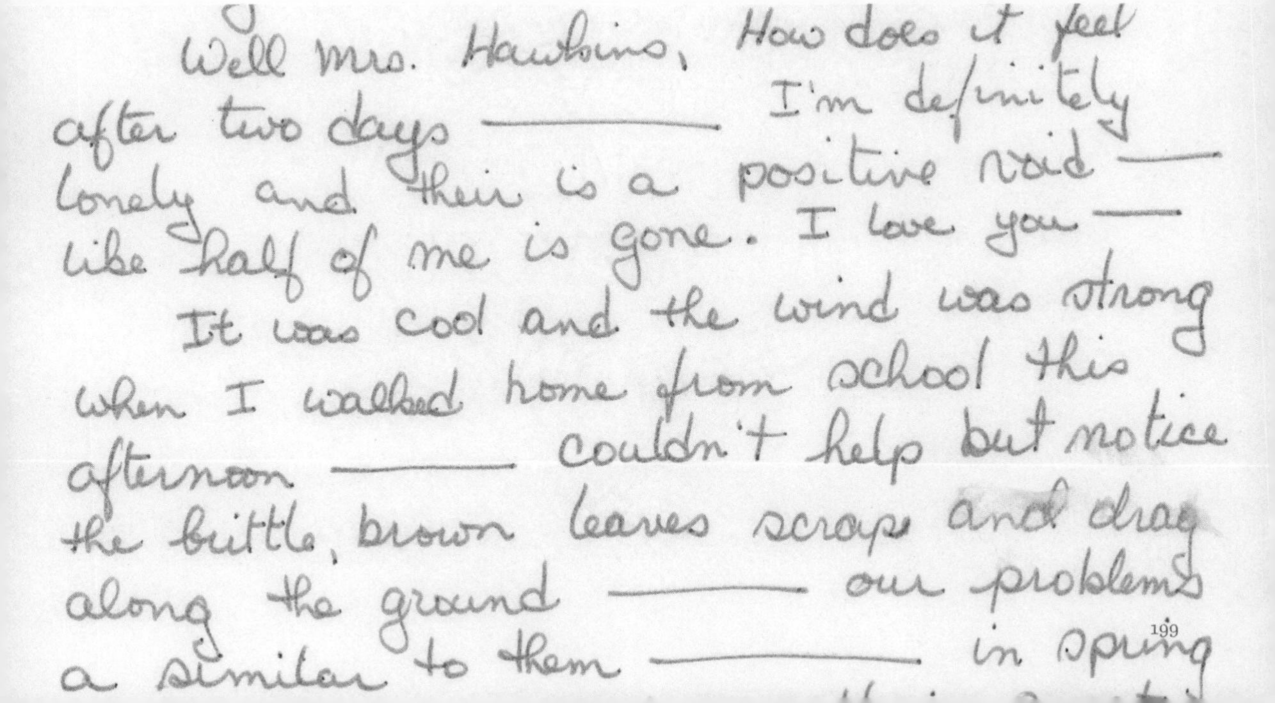
Well Mrs. Hawkins, How does it feel after two days ——— I'm definitely lonely and their is a positive void — like half of me is gone. I love you —

It was cool and the wind was strong when I walked home from school this afternoon ——— couldn't help but notice the brittle, brown leaves scrape and drag along the ground ——— our problems a similar to them ——— in spring

The weather was perfect the day I left for three weeks to sing with the Christ Church Choir of Girls and Men in Italy and Switzerland in June 1984. The bus was already in the church parking lot when my mom, dad, and I pulled up, a few other choristers and their parents already standing around. There is no doubt the trip would have been relevant to my life story even if my father had not handed me a letter in a semi-mysterious fashion just before we boarded the bus to the airport, saying, "I hope you have a marvelous time. Wait until you're on the plane to read this." But I am also sure that the letter opened me to a richer, more meaningful experience than I would have had without it.

I waited until the plane was quiet, with most all of the passengers, my friends included, trying to sleep sitting upright in the post-dinner-airplane-dark. I opened the ivory-colored envelope addressed to me to find blue ballpoint ink on seven pages of ivory-colored heavy-weight watermarked laid paper, the kind used for résumés and other business correspondence. His hand was the same one I had always known, curved and unlike any other parent's, particularly different than my mother's precise Catholic school penmanship. The moment was noteworthy, heavy with import; I cried a little.

In this letter, he opens directly, "From the time we found out you would be making this trip, I wanted to tell you everything I experienced living there." So as not to bore me with "the 'I remember . . .' bit" before I left, he writes to tell me that there are "some things I can't let escape your experience."

I'm nearly forty the first time I ask my father about art. What it is. What it means. What's

In total, there are six such things. The first has to do with visiting the stairwell outside the Duomo in Siena, where St. Catherine is said to "have fallen and lost her teeth when she was chased by the devil." The second offers directions, including a small drawing, regarding how to find the cappuccino stand in the Piazza del Campo, where he, eighteen years prior, spent a great deal of time between classes and after school. The third includes the address of the family he lived with while there, 17 Via Isozzo, and he asks me to try to locate the son, get his phone number and/or contact information. Item four instructs me to rub the nose of the lion in the Uffizi Gallery in Florence because, he tells me, "It means you'll return one day." In number five he reveals his own particular brand of humor, warning me about the pigeons, "Amazingly, they rarely shit on visitors. Other than that small grace (frankly a bare civility) they are prone to anything a 10 oz, two-legged, feathered creature might accomplish." He ends the section here with a directive: "Kill a pidgeon in Venice for me." I laughed aloud reading this passage the first time. In number six, he tells me I'll love Switzerland, closes with, "Love from the old traveler, dad," before ending with a P.S. that asks me to bring him back a rock because "All of my things from Siena were ruined when the basement flooded and this time I'd like something water won't hurt."

I read the letter over and over during the trip and followed each and every one of his directions the best I could. I think I found the right staircase, and I brought him a rock, but was unsuccessful in locating his host family. I never did kill a pigeon. I am not sure I loved Switzerland, but I did enjoy

Love

important. Why he loves it. "What," I say, "do I most need to know?" "All art boils down to three

201

it very much. Most importantly, though we never did go to the Uffizi, and I never saw any lion, I did rub the nose of the sixteenth-century bronze boar that sits in the Mercato Nuovo, the statue most websites indicate as the magical means by which one ensures both good luck and a return to Florence.

Nine years later, I returned to Italy to work as a nanny at Spannocchia, one of the many places we stayed during that first choir trip. I arrived on April 29, the feast day of St. Catherine of Siena, and lived there through July. While there, my father wrote to me once.

This letter is typed, though the address and return are written in what I recognize as his professional ASID (American Society for Interior Designers) certified all-caps drafting lettering, rather than his usual quirky cursive hand. He writes from the cottage in Port Austin, Michigan, the place he lives, or rather hides out, for a couple years post-divorce, blowing through his share of the profit made after the sale of both the building in which my parents ran the interior design business and the Whittier house.

This second letter composed on strikingly similar paper (soft white, watermarked, laid) contains fewer words, yet communicates far more than the first. In the upper left-hand corner, he offers some uncharacteristically geometric graphic drawing and opens with bathroom humor, this time personal and human rather than public and bird, hoping that since I had been there a few weeks already, I ought to have returned to

things," he tells me. "Line. Color. Design. Which, of course, are everything. Because these are the

a life of "social civility which does not include excusing yourself every hour while you deal with the change." No advice this time. No asks. No directions. Instead, he moves suddenly toward unexpected honesty, reveals uncharacteristic generosity in both reflection and thought:

> *I hope you are enjoying yourself. I think the happiest moments in my life were spent in that area. I never felt as free or as absorbed with life itself. Something about the rolling hills of Tuscany, leading from one adventure to another, wrapped me in a secret with my environment I have never known since. The stacks of hay were as wondrous as any 11th century Romanesque church and an old woman in black showed as much life in her leathered face as forty pages of Dante. To me it was a culture as different as my left hand is from my right—it was part of me I knew. How or when, I've no idea. But I always felt at home there. I wish for you a similar experience. Times change, but land remains the same and its magic is still there for the taking.*

I experience little emotion any time I reread the seven-page list-letter, though I remember well that moment of my own childhood, feel fondly for the man I knew, then, as Dad. I never remember receiving or initially reading this second letter, but now each time I read it I am often overcome with emotion. Not because my father is dead or that our relationship ended on a decidedly sour note. This reflection reveals the pleasure he experienced during four brief months in Italy. It is unusually honest. It is a seam. It is the space between two pressed palms. His left, my right.

things, you understand, that are always only kind of taught. Because, you know, they always

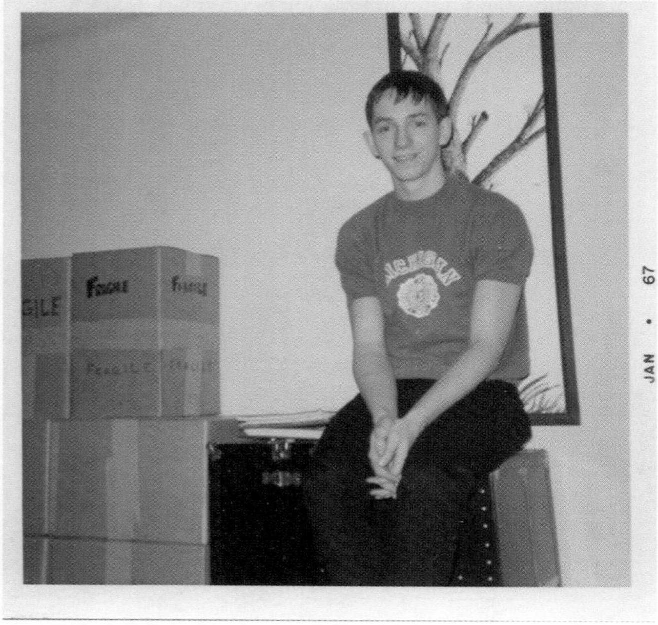

FRAGILE
FRAGILE
JAN • 67

both are and are not things we—artists—are even able to learn."

Sometime before they met, my father painted a tree on a piece of substrate my mother recently described as "something like a piece of drywall, but not exactly. Not canvas. Not wood." The tree painting appears in two of my favorite photographs of him sitting on a stack of boxes shortly before or after a move, two pictures stamped Jan 67, two images I conflated until recently when I went looking for "it" only to discover a "them."

In one, he wears a short-sleeved gray sweatshirt with the word "Michigan" in an arc over the University of Michigan seal. He's smiling fairly broadly, looking directly into the camera, sitting on the uprighted end of a steamer trunk. The tree painting is mostly behind him, but you can still see the branches sticking out from behind his head. The other image documents this similar moment yet offers a much wider frame. His feet are visible in this one, turned inward, wearing Weejuns. We can see the entire wall of boxes. His smile is mouth closed, and he's framed next to, rather than in front of, the tree. It's clear they are packing, getting ready to move. The boxes are stacked. The tree painting remains on the wall, one of the last things to come down before being put into the truck.

I know I looked at these pictures hundreds of times but never saw the image there, definitely thought nothing about it until a few years ago, when talking with my mother I offered to her that I was really mystified by the fact that he would make so much art and then somehow always destroy it, burn it, set himself up to have it destroyed or stolen. I couldn't recall this kind of violence in my childhood. Was this, I wanted to know, recent behavior, happening only after the divorce?

She listened as I worked through these ideas and considered what another artist friend had offered: "Some artists save and keep absolutely everything, others make and then destroy or abandon; completely move on." Suddenly, she said:

> Your father painted a tree. Four or five feet high. It was beautiful. I loved it. One day I came home from work and wanted to know where it was. "I destroyed it," he told me. I told him I loved that painting, that I really wished he hadn't. He looked at me and said, "Everything isn't about you. It's me. I made it, I can destroy it."

I wonder: Did my father "not exactly regret" having me and my brother because we were the art he would never be able to destroy? Maybe this is too dramatic.

And, then again, maybe this is what it means to be a parent. When you have children—however they come into your life—while you are always able to make and do more, you are also, for various unarticulatable and unknowable reasons, simultaneously always-ever unable to go on to something else.

14 / September 28, 1966

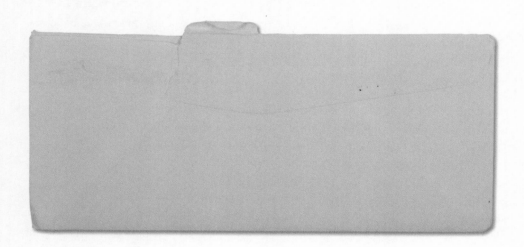

HAWKINS - 139 Fordham Dr,
Buffalo, N.y
14216
BUFFALO
SEP 29
PM
1966
N.Y.
8¢
U.S. AIR MAIL
Tricia Brien
722 South Forest
Ann Arbor, Michigan

constantly with you ——

Giorgio

We were driving to my mother's house when
I asked my brother what he remembered
of the time that our father burned most all
his belongings in a bonfire after my parents
divorced.

Sometimes my brother is generous with his storytelling; this time, he was not.

"Cliff took me in," he said. "When Dad was in jail."

"That time for domestic violence? What do you mean by 'took you in'? You were older, right?" My father was arrested for a fight with a man he was dating, a fight that became incredibly loud and got pretty out of control.

"Yeah. He had to wait to bail himself out. I was nineteen, twenty, I guess. Cliff fed me, and I hung out there."

Cliff was a family friend who owned the Lucky Horseshoe Motel, a series of small cabins placed around a horse-shoe-shaped driveway in Port Austin, Michigan. There was no fencing separating the backyards between the motel and what was once the cottage owned by my parents, the house where my father then lived and my brother was staying. My brother didn't continue, and so I took a different tack.

"How do you bail yourself out?"

"You wait until you see the judge. They release you on your own free will."

"You mean your recognizance, that you're cool unless you do something to fuck things up for yourself."

"Yeah, Dad didn't have no bail money. Neither did I. It was five thousand dollars, or some shit." My brother explained that domestic violence arrests always involve really high bail.

"So, then what happened when he got out?"

"He came back that night and dug a hole in the backyard and then went to bed. The next morning, he started bringing all kinds of shit out of the house and then lit it on fire."

"What was in there?" I was pressing now, but I really wanted to see it, to be able to picture this pyre.

"All kinds of shit."

"Do you remember anything in particular?"

"Fuck no!" He was angry, but then took a breath. "I don't know. Furniture, a bunch of paintings he did. Just stuff. Lots of shit. It was fucking big."

Two years before this exchange with my brother, four years before he died, I had asked my father about the bonfire. He offered his own similarly stripped-down version of the story. "I had made a series of self-portraits," he told me. "I burned them all."

Years after the bonfire, but before my father's death, I asked my mother what she knew of the fire: "Your father was very, very angry with me. And so, he told me that he burned everything. Anything I had ever touched."

love

shall head for my womb

..e "z's", but not without

how much I'm in love with

——— Someday we'll have

..ow's to yub in the days

.n ourselves at night. I

.'t feel for this temporary

mrs. H., especially after

marriage ——— guess I

real shit!!!!! I love you

constantly with you

Giorgio

Because Natalia Danesi Murray offers the reader her own thoughts, fills in space between letters, narrates interactions between herself and Janet Flanner, presenting intimate details such as where they vacationed and how they managed their time apart, I didn't much care that *Darlinghissima: Letters to a Friend* never presents letters from Murray to Flanner. I honored the literary power of their omission, wondering whether they were excluded because she no longer had them, or because she didn't want her own writing revealed, or because she didn't want to overshadow her dedication to, and regard for, Janet's words. I was curious to know, if she did have them at the time of publishing, whether she thought of them as belonging to Janet, who, then dead, had no way of giving permission to put them into print. The exclusion, I decided, could be for any combination of these reasons, and I am, for the most part, content with Murray's explanation for making Flanner's letters to her available for all to see:

> I hope my grandchildren, and other young men and women like them, born in a freerer, more liberated society, more knowledgeable about relationships between the sexes and without the inhibitions or taboos of an earlier era, will understand and value our experience and efforts to be, above all, decent human beings. This is the intention of this book.

Neither woman ever used the word "lesbian" or "gay" or "queer" to describe themselves, yet here is a stated desire for a legacy of relationship, relevance spelled out about thirty years before same-sex marriage is made legal in thirty-five states by court decision, state legislature, or popular vote. This intention framed in the introduction of the volume is bookended by the harrowing story of Janet's final evening of life, of Natalia's being denied access to her beloved, left to wait in a hospital hallway, far away from the family waiting rooms, for the announcement of Janet's death. The poignancy, the simplicity, the stark reality of this moment lands heavy on the final page:

> At daybreak, a man began to wash the floors. Then the day nurses began to appear. At six a.m. a man approached us. It was the anesthetist. "The heart failed," he announced as a matter of fact. Without further words, he handed me a bundle: pyjamas and the red robe; all that was left of my Janet.

Maybe this is why I so wish I could get my hands on one—just one—of these letters. Whatever it is Natalia wrote to Janet that compelled her to then craft this missive of December 31, 1958:

My darling love,

Thank you for the most beautiful and complete love letter I have ever known in my life, larger and more illuminating on the meaning of the structure of love in a curiously lived life, as you lead and know yours, than any I have read, too, in poetry or memoirs. Stendhal's little volume on "Love," with its frequently trumpery incidents and, it is true, the flashes of his masculine losses which gave wisdom of comment, is poor fare compared to the analysis of emotion you gave to me. This is not merely complimentary, and you know that. This is profoundly deep appreciation for your thoughts and their application on this great human subject on which, as I have often told you, each fortunate human talks privately in the early happiest love-period or experience of existence, but pitifully little has been recorded of stated importance. This you have achieved. I shall never forget this letter or lose it. It is the major apogee of the reception of the gift of emotion in my long life. I cannot in any way express my love for you in an equality of discovery and appreciation, except to tell you that I know that what you wrote is the truth, rarely approached, but seized by you in its significance as your own definition of your own significant deep nature.

What if this letter exists? Could it possibly match up to the praise, adoration, and admiration Janet communicates here?

I wrote to the archivists at the National Archive in Washington, DC, where the Janet Flanner and Natalia Danesi Murray Papers are housed, and was told that there are no letters from Natalia to Janet in the December 1958 file. There are, as stated in the "Finding Aid to the Collection in the Library of Congress," a few letters from Natalia to Janet, but I have not traveled to see for myself. The more I think about this letter, the more comfort I find in being limited to consideration of its once-upon-a-time existence. And as the comfort accumulates, the more I believe that Natalia's letter is best left to my imagination, to the seam, to the realm of the asemic, an image of a letter written in non-referential text, the wordless aesthetic impression of language. We all have an image of what the perfect love letter would be. I am content to allow Janet's perfect letter to become mine, imagined in and as body, rendered and re-membered on and as the page.

She almost didn't get on the plane, but that seemed mean and a bit of an overreaction. There was no reason not to go just because she was having second thoughts. No reason not to spend a lovely weekend together. All during the flight she thought about how she would tell him. Just because they had already bought rings didn't mean they couldn't decide to return to the original plan and wait until June. They weren't even going to the town hall until tomorrow. There was still plenty of time to think about it, time to talk. Plenty of space to reconsider this decision and use the weekend to just be together rather than worry about getting married right this minute. It wasn't cold feet, she would reassure him, but maybe this wasn't the best time after all.

She heard them before she saw them, two men cheering and clapping as she stepped off the Jetway and into the Buffalo International Airport. The last time she arrived, he was there alone. If he had come alone, there might have been an opening for this conversation. But this time he had brought along his best friend, Tom. Perhaps it was more accurate to say the best friend had brought him; it was, after all, Tom's car.

Her moment of doubt was subsumed by their energy and enthusiasm; it was impossible not to smile as soon as she saw them both. Tom approached her first, warmly wrapping his arms around her before swaying their momentarily fused torsos in two quick side-to-side movements before releasing her abruptly, spinning to his friend to say, "Well, don't let me get in the way of you two love birds!"

Though it was more her speed, she didn't find the embrace with her fiancé—a word that still somehow didn't feel right—especially reassuring. But in the press and pulse of their bodies, she felt her arguments retreat, her resolve erode. This wasn't a decision based on what she wanted, but it isn't that she didn't want him either. Not exactly. When the not wanting is more powerful than the wanting—not wanting to be a teacher, not wanting her mother to die, not wanting there to be conflict about a wedding—it can be incredibly difficult to know what to do.

From that point forward, the weekend was a blur. His other three roommates were there to greet her when they got back to the house. Beer and fried chicken; cigarette smoking and cards into the night. The next day five of them piled into a car and drove to Eden, New York, of all places, to have the ceremony performed by the justice of the peace. She in a wool granny-apple-green dress, which she very much liked. He in a black suit and tie, which she liked equally well. In a matter of minutes, they made a commitment to be together for the rest of their years.

She didn't seem to relax until a few hours before she was to leave. She lay awake next to him as he slept, listening to the rise and fall of his chest, sounds she decided could become as familiar and dependable as she wanted. If she listened just the right way, she could hear the waves of the ocean in each inhale-exhale, and from this space imagine them again standing on the beach as they had earlier that summer, relocating the freedom she had felt.

First light came in as fractals, the sun seeping through the fall leaves on the trees outside. She watched the light silently dance on the wall, uninterrupted by drapeless panes. On this wall he had hung a series of his own paintings, each one signed as he signed his letters: Giorgio. Her favorite of them all was what appeared to be a dead, leafless tree. The black-on-white image was larger than any other piece on the wall, almost as tall as she was. She liked the mood it set: stark, clear, and severe.

She studied his strokes; the ways straight lines could collectively create the illusion of a rounded branch. She didn't know whether he had done it in oils or acrylics. She only knew that he was recently practicing working with India ink. She could see the point of view was from below and imagined she was lying under that tree. The painted tree had no leaves, but she could see them in the shadows made by the tree outside, its canopy moving across the ceiling and down the wall, onto the branches of his image, over them both. This, a gorgeous co-creation, his tree and her leaves, in the continuous dapple dance of shadow and sun.

My father moved into a room in our house on December 1, 2006. The nineteenth World AIDS Day. In the first thirty-six hours following arrival, he transformed a 10×12 room most completely. In the room, he placed a twin bed, a French chair, a step stool, a bookshelf, a large dresser, a small dresser, a bedside table, two lamps, a small space heater, a plant stand, a plant, an area rug, and a television. The walls held at least a dozen pieces of art, and he was not yet done hanging. Decorative objects such as a black lacquered box, a marble obelisk, and brass meditation chimes occupied much of the limited surface area. On the bookshelf next to the black metal sculpture of Mercury/Hermes, he had an amaryllis. Every object, every piece, was placed with purpose and intention.

In the first thirty days my father lived with us, he began and worked on thirty different projects, some of which were completed, many of which were not. Though he had ostensibly come there to die, with each passing day, his health improved. Hopelessness and helplessness lifted just a bit more with each stitch, each knot; each bead he'd thread, every stroke he would make. It wasn't until I witnessed his inability to hold a needle and thread, see no visible progress on the quilt that was on his lap during the visits I made the last few weeks of his life, that I realized that though he appeared unwell at the time, in 2006 he was nowhere near death. He was figuring out how to transition from working person to nonworking person. He was making. He was transforming stress over his deteriorating body into desire accessed through a body of work.

What little of his work now remains can mostly be categorized in the area of textile and fiber arts: quilts, runners, needlepoint, embroidery, tatting, crochet. Some pieces, such as the runner with a cigar-printed fabric he once made for me as a Christmas gift, are completed. Many, such as numerous needlepoint projects and his AIDS quilt, are not. The year following his death, my mother paid to have someone complete for me the partial afghan he was crocheting made with gorgeous, expensive, richly colored variegated yarn. I am in a slow, considered years-long, process of thinking through how, when, and, in some cases, whether to complete the many partially crafted pieces. To date, I have sent two quilts to a quilter to be bound so they can be hung in my home. I am more puzzled by what to do with incomplete needlepoint projects. Shall I carry out what appears to have been the plan, taking up the very needle still threaded, left so mundanely mid-stitch it could have been left there only last night? Or do I mark myself there, too, and turn away from his artistic intentions, offer my own aesthetic vision, and become an uninvited collaborator in the work?

What interests me most is that whether finished or not, my father's skill and talent are evident in each piece that remains. His piecing and machine stitching are just shy of meticulous. Artistic and purposeful, but not overworked. The fabric choices and color combinations—often pink-forward and chintz-centric—are signature George. Surer, but not unlike the handwriting and some of the drawings in the letters to my mother, his embroidery handiwork reveals a particular ability to pair, combine, and assemble straight stitches in order to create the illusion of curved lines.

love

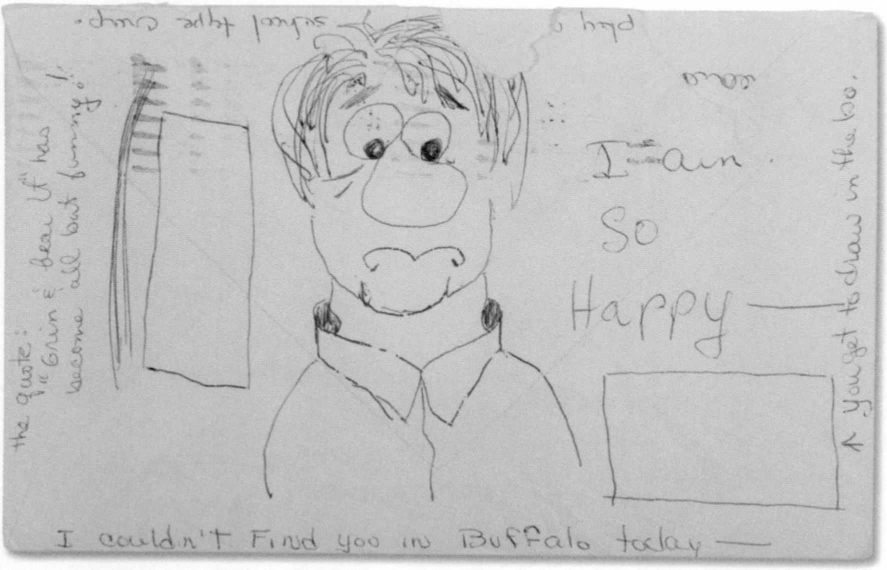
I am
So
Happy—
I couldn't Find you in Buffalo today—
You get to draw in the box.

BUFFALO, N.Y.
PM
29 SEP
1966
28
8¢
U.S. AIR MAIL
Tricia O'Brien
722 South Forest
Ann Arbor, Michigan

Friends—

I write to let you know that George F. Hawkins (b. September 7, 1944), took his last breath on April 18, 2011 at 5:10 pm. Those who knew George well can attest that the gift he gave to the world, the source of his human grace, was a reverence for beauty and particular regard for visual elegance. Flowers and fabric remained his passion to the end; it wasn't until he was physically unable to manipulate a needle, to arrange a bouquet, that he began his decline. It has been a privilege to witness my father's transition from life to death this past week. To behold rose-stem veins in his forearms and hands become bits of lilac and pewter colored embroidery floss beneath organza skin.

Many have asked, "What can I do for you?" in an effort to illustrate their love and support for our family. It isn't, I've come to realize, what you can do for us that is relevant at this moment. Over the past twelve days, the sum total of his nursing home residency, I realized that we can best honor George by honoring ourselves, by regarding the things he revered. In that spirit, I offer these suggestions:

1) Plant flowers for yourself or someone else.

2) Clean out your closets and basements and storage spaces and donate gently and rarely used items to resale shops. (In Chicago, I highly recommend Howard Brown's Brown Elephant Stores: http://www.howardbrown.org/.)

3) Buy a bouquet for yourself or someone else.

4) Donate time or money to Test-Positive Aware Network (T-PAN: http://www.tpan.com/) HIV/AIDS support services.

5) Tell a ridiculous, over-the-top—a 'bedazzled'—story.

6) Eat some cake.

I want to close by relaying my gratitude to the nursing and support staff on the second floor of The Grove in LaGrange Park, as well as the amazing individuals we encountered through Unity Hospice. It was a pleasure to get to know each and every one of the remarkable individuals who took care of my father in his final days. I remind you all to be sure that whenever you find yourself in similar circumstances that you make sure to look at and not through, speak with and never only to, the caregivers of this world.

Thanks to you all for your thoughts, love, prayers, and intentions.

Sincerely,

Ames

love

Letter #16, found, sent, and postmarked September 29, was actually written on September 21. Had it been mailed when intended, I would have ordered it as Letter #11 or #12 in the set. As it happens, I have ordered them not as they were written but as they were received. In this smallest of actions, there is the privileging of the reader/unmaker over the writer/maker, an alignment with the reader, my mother, the person for whom the letters were written.

I was recently asked whether I would ever reproduce these letters in their entirety. I never intend to do so. In so many ways, they say so little; in other ways, they reveal too much. In a love letter, we work hard, in the best way we know how, to convince someone else to have us, to love us, to want us the way we want them. We have the opportunity to reinvent and reimagine a new self on the page. Even then, the love letter does its best work when we are working on how it is we want to have ourselves, love ourselves, want ourselves the way we already are.

My father made creative and considerable use of profanity, often when he was doing something like pruning, arranging flowers, recovering a chair, decorating a Christmas tree, packing the car. When he was frustrated by the ways his body impeded him, when he wanted to be able to move faster, do more, hold more. When space, time, and materials weren't in concert with, and at the complete beck and call of, his hands.

I can't say he never raised his middle finger, but I don't remember this being a usual or preferred expression for him. I don't recall him using the word "fuck," or any of the words or phrases that include it, though I wouldn't claim he never did. He preferred "shit" and "goddammit" and "sonofabitch." Curses that never used to, but now seem to, mark him as being of a different time. The time before computers and cable. When he would swear in holy family: *Jesus, Mary, and Joseph!* When I learned that the Lord—*Jesus H. Christ*—had a middle name.

The day before my father would never open his eyes again, he was still able to mostly sit up, but not quite straight, as he listed obviously toward the left side. He spoke, but I couldn't quite hear him. His voice had faded many decibels below a whisper, and I wasn't trying to read his lips. I was watching his arms. Watching them move in ways that now appeared as imprecise copies, glitchy digitizations, of what his limbs used to be able to do. He was not quite strong enough to wield their weight, and a sweeping wrist flourish occasionally resulted in the sudden plummet of his hands toward the blanket, birds diving for fish. The third time this happened, he snagged a weeks-old wound, an eighth-inch split into the tip of his thumb. It wasn't open, but never healed, having peeled into a permanent V of hardened, calloused skin.

It took some effort to understand that he wanted me to hand him the emery board, one of the few objects he had in his bedside table. I watched him concentrate hard to execute a few unidirectional strokes across calcified skin. When he didn't swear after missing his target a third, then fourth, then fifth time, I pressed my fingers all together, breathed in sour air, and silently fisted *fuck*.

I love you   I love you   I love you
love you
        I love you   I love you
I love you
    I love you   I love you
                I love you
I love you   I love you
I love you   I love you
                        I love you
    I love you
I love you   I love you   I love you
                I love you

LOVE   YOU
        I love you
love you   I love you   I love you
I love you   I love you
                I love you   I love you
        I love you
I love you   I love you   I love you   229

It felt like magical serendipity when, deep in the course of writing this book, I learned that Vita Sackville-West's son Nigel Nicolson referred to *Orlando* by Virginia Woolf as "the longest and most charming love letter in literature." I had not yet read *Orlando*, but I had read the letters between Virginia and Vita. The two women met at a dinner party in mid-December 1922. Though there is evidence to suggest that each was intensely drawn to the other from the start, their relationship didn't intensify until mid-1924 when Virginia and her husband, Leonard, invited Vita to write a novel for their newly created Hogarth Press. Vita gladly accepted the request, writing, "You asked me to write a story for you. On the peaks of mountains and beside green lakes, I am writing it for you." *Seducers in Ecuador* becomes the first of more than a dozen volumes published by Hogarth Press. *Orlando*, it seemed to me, was not the only codex love letter in the relationship.

Here, in this space created by the acceptance of an invitation to write, an affair between these two women writers begins. It is an affair chronicled in hundreds of letters, ones that document a physical relationship but, perhaps more importantly, reveal a shared passion for writing as a constant force in their bond. It is on the occasion of facing writer's block that Virginia claims to discover *Orlando* as a possible remedy for her "despair." On October 9, 1927, in the wake of her success with *To the Lighthouse*, Virginia writes:

> Yesterday morning I was in despair: . . . I couldn't screw a word from me; and at last dropped my head in my hands: dipped my pen in the ink, and wrote these words, as if automatically, on a clean sheet: Orlando: A Biography. No sooner had I done this than my body was flooded with rapture and my brain with ideas. I wrote rapidly till 12 . . . But, listen; suppose Orlando turns out to be Vita; and it's all about you and the lusts of your flesh and the lure of your mind (heart you have none, who go gallivanting down the lanes with Campbell) . . . Shall you mind? Say yes, or No: . . .

Two days later, without any attention to Virginia calling out her affair with Mary Campbell, Vita enthusiastically replies, "My God, Virginia, if ever I was thrilled and terrified it is at the prospect of being projected

love

into the shape of Orlando." Vita acknowledges, "What fun for you, what fun for me," and notes, "any vengeance that you ever want to take will lie ready to your hand," and yet still makes clear: "You have my full permission." The only condition being that, "whatever it is that you intend to do, you ought to dedicate it to your victim." Of course, she does.

I do not recall exactly where I was when I first began reading *Orlando*, but I know exactly where I was when I first read the scene in chapter three when Orlando (following a weeklong sleep during a riot in Constantinople, where he relocated to escape his broken heart following his affair with a Russian princess and to narrowly escape a rebound relationship with Archduchess Harriet) via a magical, deus ex machina moment, following a dreamlike sequence complete with the siren/angel figures of Lady of Purity, Lady of Chastity, and Lady of Modesty and the obligatory, if predictable, trumpets that blare, "The Truth and nothing but the Truth," shifts from man to woman in his-turned-her thirtieth year. At a picnic table at Red Door Brewing in Albuquerque, New Mexico, in early May 2015, I wrenched myself from the page following the final, "terrific blast:—'The Truth!' at which Orlando awoke." I stared out past the beer in front of me, fixating on the crushed gravel, feeling the sliver of late afternoon sun on my neck, noticing again the trace of cedar and mesquite in the air. "Orlando had become a woman—there's no denying it," Woolf writes. "But in every other respect, Orlando remained precisely as he had been. The change of sex, though it altered their future, did nothing whatever to alter their identity."

When *does* a book become a love letter? The moment Orlando awakens as a woman. The woman that she was. The woman with this history as a man, a man with a future as a woman. A not-man who was, because of a trans-trance experience, a woman. A book becomes a love letter when a muse is not simply inspiration but an addressee. When, because of Virginia, because of Vita, because of the words they exchanged and shared so many years before, ones written in love and passion for writing and each other, Orlando as man, woman, and writer, as a Virginia-Vita co-creation, awakens. And as a result, so may I.

Letters are "made" from bits and pieces of our own lived life—our experiences, our memories, our stories. They reflect personal preference for language, vocabulary, word combinations, idiomatic structures, and cultural sayings. Letters are often expressions of a self that moves between a state of comfort and confusion, concrete and sublime. The letter pushes toward internal horizons, offering a means of reorienting the self. Letters are also "unmade" when they are read. Literal decoding concurrent with processes of comprehension and sense making guide us to consider not only what was said but what the recipient imagines was also/may have been intended.

The questions we might ask ourselves as letter writers: How do we choose to make use of the form of letter? How do we let ourselves be seen? To what degree is letter writing an exercise in using language to show ourselves who we have, might, are willing to become? The reader's questions always mirrored in response: How much room has been left for us in this letter? Does this letter make us feel as though we have been seen? How much space is there in which we can imagine ourselves to be?

I am never far from this thought: In reading these letters, the young woman who will become my mother unmade the world and the initial intentions of the young man who will become my father. She took whatever it is he offered and remade meaning for herself. When she saved them, she engaged in the creation of a collection. In giving them to me she unmade their relevance for herself again, offering another opportunity of meaning making to me. Here, they are again unmade, remade, repurposed, and transformed. Twenty renditions of twenty letters exploring how love might be written in life, might be read on the page. Twenty ways to re-create my father's hand in mine; honor my mother's hands as they opened and held and saved these letters. You, Dear Reader, are also here, you know, in the most sacred of roles, left to read and consider what has been offered in terms of whatever you have read, and loved for and of yourself, both on and off the page.

Your own experience, Dear Reader, is what you have been handed.
It's (the something that is at) the heart of this book.

thing that lets them know
I'm still alright & my type
of normal (er, rather out type)
is that I'm still not making
any sense and they don't
understand me _____

All my love for all the
        long times in the world —

                Giorgio

Say Hi to Romer for me!

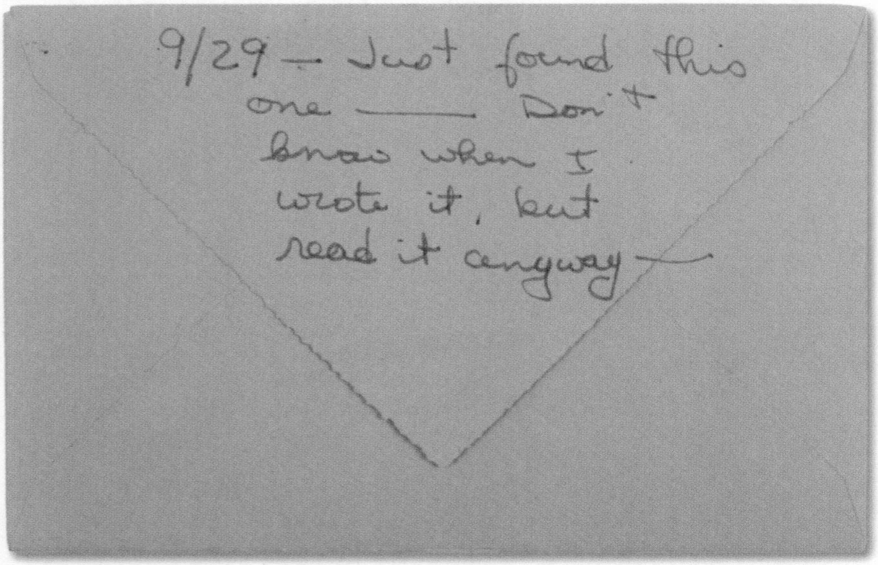
9/29 — Just found this
one —— Don't
know when I
wrote it, but
read it anyway —

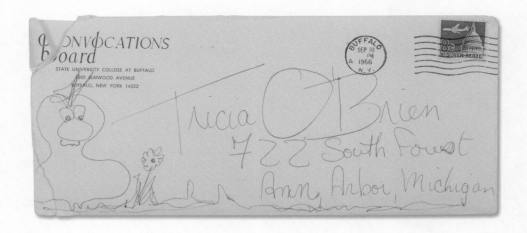

Tricia O'Brien
722 South Forest
Ann Arbor, Michigan

CONVOCATIONS Board
STATE UNIVERSITY COLLEGE AT BUFFALO
1300 ELMWOOD AVENUE
BUFFALO, NEW YORK 14222

BUFFALO
SEP 30
PM
A 1966
N.Y.

U.S. AIR MAIL

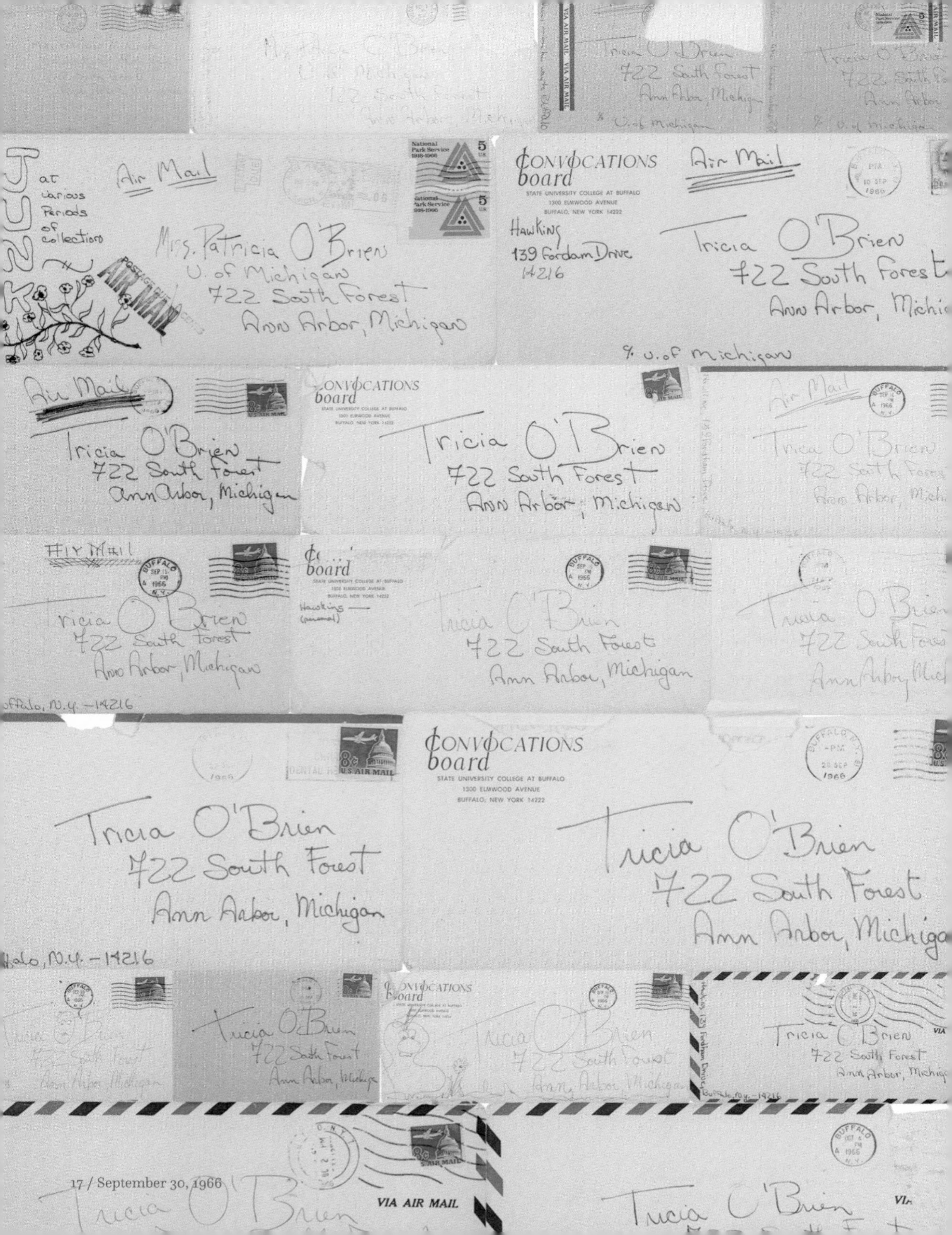
Mrs. Patricia O'Brien
U. of Michigan
722 South Forest
Ann Arbor, Michigan
Tricia O'Brien
722 South Forest
Ann Arbor, Michigan
% U. of Michigan
at various Periods of collections
Air Mail
National Park Service 1916-1966
CONVOCATIONS board
STATE UNIVERSITY COLLEGE AT BUFFALO
1300 ELMWOOD AVENUE
BUFFALO, NEW YORK 14222
Hawkins
139 Fordam Drive
14216
Hawkins (personal)
Buffalo, N.Y. – 14216
U.S. AIR MAIL
VIA AIR MAIL

17 / September 30, 1966

The quick pop of fear that blithely faded into weighty sadness the first moment I saw my father in the nursing home came again when I saw his partially gutted apartment; a second hollowing. But, the apartment was quiet, the day was wet and cold, and I settled into the dependability of this melancholy through the necessary actions of sorting and packing.

I surveyed the space in earnest, strategizing how to triage the remainder of his belongings. First, I discarded the garbage, the actual surface trash left behind; mundane bits of flotsam denoting recent human presence. I picked up the last coffee-stained napkin he'd ever create. For a moment, just a flash, I considered saving it, tracing it, needlepointing it, a way of somehow preserving one of his final moments of animation.

The coffee rings reminded me of a visit with him in the nursing home five days prior, when he was agitated, distressed by the bird lady who, he claimed, wouldn't free the birds from their cage. He kept leaning forward, pointing to the wall just below the TV that was never, in his twelve-day stay, turned on. He asked me to help him keep his glasses on, trying, it turns out, to get a better look. "Dad," I asked, not knowing what else to say, "how do you feel?" He turned his head so abruptly that I flinched inside and braced myself for paternal rage. But he hadn't turned toward me as my father, deliberate and ready to admonish. He had turned to the world as its queen, eyes sparkly fabulous, widely fey. Taking as deep a breath as he was able, he spoke to the space beyond me, and in a clear breathy toothless lisp uttered what I now know to be his final flourish: "Did you see that crazy-ass parade last night?"

Alone in his space, alone with what now remained of his stuff, I started feeling as close to him as I ever had. Tenderness seeped in below the surface of my skin as I touched the remaining items in turn, considering his matter as my matter, as that which has both never and always mattered.

— Really enjoyed your call. Had no news to tell, but could sit for hrs. telling you about nothings....... above our love —— I just enjoy talking to you ——

— must stop writing now as I'm really upset as the cleaners just called and they seemed to have lost $40 worth of my pants —— I'm really pissed!!!!!!!!! ——

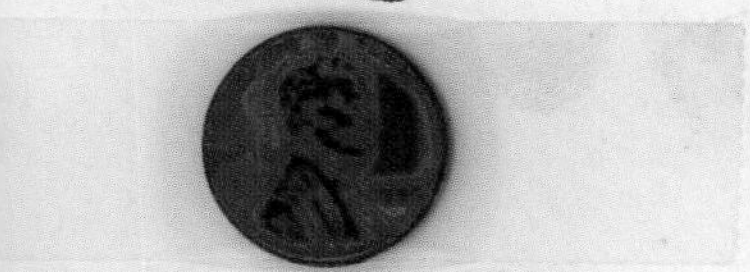

Yep I'm back!!!

Forgot to give you this "lucky penny" that I found while walking home from school yesterday... It's what you get for walking along with your nose to the ground as I do —— you'll note how "lucky" it is as it has my birth year on it!!

love

It occurs to me, during my fifth or sixth read-through of Letter #17, that this one sounds and feels the most like a real love letter. This isn't because the letter is full of passion or reveals physical desire for my mother, though he does, for the first time, directly mention rather than simply allude to the fact that my parents were having sex. He's "hornier than hell," and the distance between them is the reason that they are "a bit sparse in that area for the time being." But Giorgio intellectualizes rather than carnalizes his considerations of sex, admitting that "I was always under the assumption that there was more to marriage than sex_____." When he follows this three-inch writerly slash-pause by confirming his belief, "and after four days of marriage I am sure of it_____," I first wonder whether he writes to convince her or himself. But then I start to see the answer as neither and the lines in this letter as somehow different than the space-filling gaps between thought. These slashes feel like misplaced underscoring, offset under-linings meant to emphasize the notion that there is "more to marriage than sex," he is "sure of it." In such repositioning I hear him declare rather than pause: "I love you in so many, many ways, sex being just one."

Perhaps it isn't "the most beautiful and complete love letter," as Janet tells Natalia, but I am struck by the resonance Letter #17 has with "Stendhal's little volume," *On Love*, his more than 350-page 1822 tome. It has been said that of his more than twenty different volumes, which include genres such as novels, novellas, and biography, Stendhal was most proud of *On Love*. Inspired by an instance of unrequited love, one that must have been incredibly powerful given the scope of the work, *On Love* spans three different books, the first of which he claims to be a "scientific" (read neutral) observation of the processes of falling and being in love. The second organizes thoughts through a nationalist lens, presenting cultural differences with respect to love across different countries in Europe, as well as Arabia and the United States. The third offers

"Scattered Fragments," a wide range of quotations, aphorisms, insular thoughts, disconnected ideas both directly and indirectly connected to the topic at hand.

While Stendhal wasn't widely read in his day, I do understand why *On Love* found readerly traction in the early twentieth century. His observations regarding the process of crystallization, "the operation of the mind which, from everything which is presented to it, draws the conclusion that there are new perfections in the object of its love," offer insight for postindustrial Western cultures working to codify, naturalize, and monetize the notion that there is one perfect person for each of us, a story undergirding the grand narrative myth of romantic love.

Stendhal's crystallization is a process largely of the mind in which the lover discovers in everything that happens proof of the perfection of the beloved. Crystallization is natural, emanating from the sensation that pleasure located in the feelings is in direct relationship to the perfection of the object of desire. Stendhal explains that we know a first crystallization has occurred if it is soon followed by doubt. Not the doubt that the lover is in love with the beloved, but the unbearable uncertainty as to whether the beloved loves the lover in return. A second crystallization ensues, which exists in the synergy of a back-and-forth process between certainty and doubt—much of which occurs in the mind of the lover—solidifying the idea that "She loves me." A fragile, if tenuous, confidence prompts in the lover the most powerful belief: they must have the beloved. The toggle here between ecstasy and uncertainty, "the path on the extreme edge of a terrible abyss and within touch, on the other hand, of perfect happiness," is that which "gives so great a superiority to the second crystallisation over the first." In establishing this belief—that the beloved is the absolute best thing that ever happened to the lover, who can be happy only if the two are forever together—comes a new desire: obtaining proof.

love

"How could you *do* that?" my brother asked once we got outside and were walking under the elevated train tracks of the Red Line after leaving my father's apartment. I'm startled by the question. Not because I don't understand why he might be asking, but because even though it had only been about an hour ago, the memory of giving my father a quarter-inch buzz cut seemed incidental to the fact that the three of us, as a family, had just gone through the intake process for my father to enter hospice. On St. Patrick's Day, no less. Not that any of us cared all that much about this drinking holiday, but the knowledge that the city was in full party mode made the day that much more surreal. "What?" I asked, though I heard what he said. "How could you get that close to him? Touch him? How did you not gag? Why would you do it?"

The smell of the cancer now growing on the outside of my father's body was so intense, so putrid, that my brother and I had used Carmex under our nostrils to try to mute the stench. I knew it was possible to acclimate to displeasing smells, but this wasn't your run-of-the-mill shit, barf, cigarette smoke, or garbage. It behaved nothing like the bouquet of skunk spray or a fart. This mephitic stink was not just strong, it was formidable. Hanging in the air like humidity, a thickly noxious olfactory weight.

The intake process with hospice was arduous and difficult, as my father, though passive and ultimately yielding, was decidedly laconic and reticent. I could have said it was the stark contrast of the clear, nearly peppy directive he gave the moment the hospice team left that compelled me to nod, grab the clippers: "OK, now, let's cut my hair." It would have been

Love

easy enough to say that I wanted to be nice, to do something loving, offer care in a way he wanted and requested. But that wasn't quite true. I could have said that I felt somewhat sorry for him, but I didn't. And though I felt guilty about many things, it's not why I cut his hair. Practically speaking, since it was chin length and getting longer, it was difficult to deal with. But, I didn't agree to cut his hair only because he was no longer able to bathe.

I agreed because I would get to do one of the things he always said he hated: have his head touched. I agreed because it provided narrative continuity for the many times he cut our hair as children, the multiple times he dyed my hair blond when I was a teen. I agreed so that, rather than enter the rage I now felt, I would be forced to be as gentle as possible. I agreed because I wanted the opportunity to gingerly lift locks up with my left hand, so his hair wouldn't catch in the less than ideally sharp blades as I slowly drew the clippers back and forth across his scalp with my right. To experience skin over skull as tenuous and fragile as the sight of a newly hatched chick, featherless, black-eyed and dead on the sidewalk. I agreed, I understood, because of the abject potential of this moment. Not in spite of, but precisely because I wanted to sidle up to, the stench.

I shrugged, jammed my hands deeper in my pockets, let a train rumble by before saying, "I don't know. I just did."

Love

Love

love

——————— In Letter #17, of love my father writes:

superior to any alive or lived . . . . maybe love is an allusion as the psychatrists say or 'doesn't exist as the existencialist preach ————— but whatever this feeling is I have I don't want to loose it — ever ————————— and I want to built it as we watch the years fold back ————————— there is no immortality to life and it only exists for the present and in years no one will ever care that we existed except for the decendents ————— but we care and love now ————————— that is more than reason for you & I to be US!

The second crystallization seems to have arrived. Love is not an illusion. It exists. Marriage becomes proof of their connection, a means by which he is able to not only express desire to maintain these love feelings but reinforce them as they together "watch the years fold back."

On the last page of this letter, I sense traces of the vacillation Stendhal notes among (1) belief that the beloved is perfect; (2) feeling that the beloved loves him; and (3) desire for proof; not in an expression of frenzy, but in the way that the elopement seems to have offered an ensuing quiet.

Love

small period of "pinch me I'm dreaming" about our wedding has left.... as I told Susan, I truly feel married (not as much as I will in June of course) and adore the feeling. The world hasn't changed and life goes on the same as it did before, but their is now a certain gentility about it than makes everything bearable. I used to wait for the bottom to drop out of everything —————— now, with you, I can only

Within the legal status of marriage, a hope for descendants, evidence of a love that is returned, one that they together co-create and share, my father considers the specter of death and his legacy. He is, in this moment, sure of his love for my mother. Sure of her love for him. Surer, it appears, than he's ever been of love at all.

life will give to me —————— when I cease to exist ———— so shall we as people forget——— but now our love is so all-encompassing that it is life unto itself ———— what could be a finer alter to mortality?

Love is all-encompassing. Love is life unto itself. Love is an altar.

Love is letters.

Letters to have. To hold. From this day forward.

Love.

Line.

Lineage.

Now and forever.

Crystallized.

love

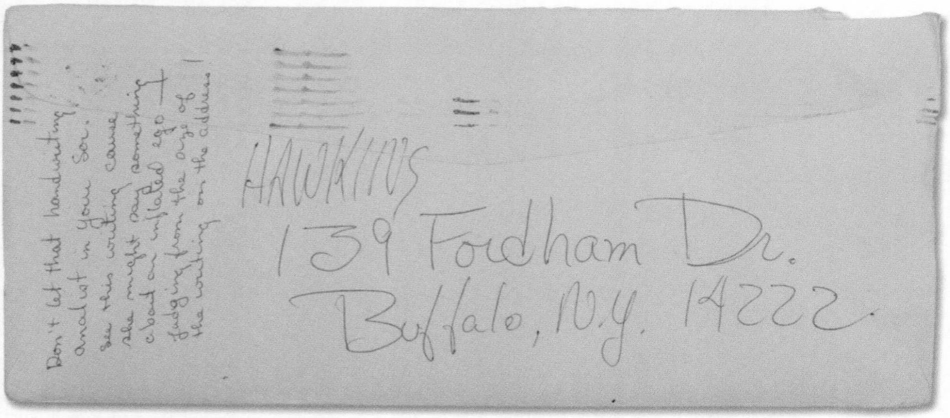
Don't let that handwriting
analist in your Soc.
see this writing cause
she might say something
about an inflated ego —
judging from the size of
the writing on the address!
HAWKINS
139 Fordham Dr.
Buffalo, N.Y. 14222

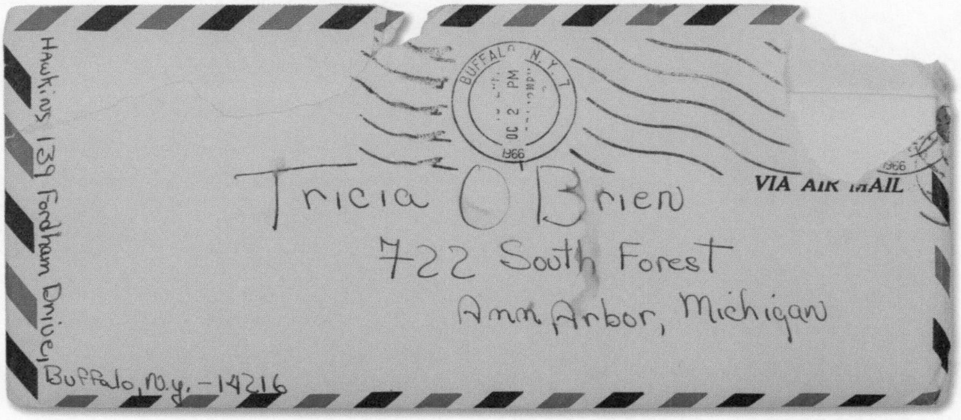
Hawkins 139 Fordham Drive, Buffalo, N.Y. -14216
BUFFALO N.Y. T
PM
1966
VIA AIR MAIL
Tricia O Brien
722 South Forest
Ann Arbor, Michigan

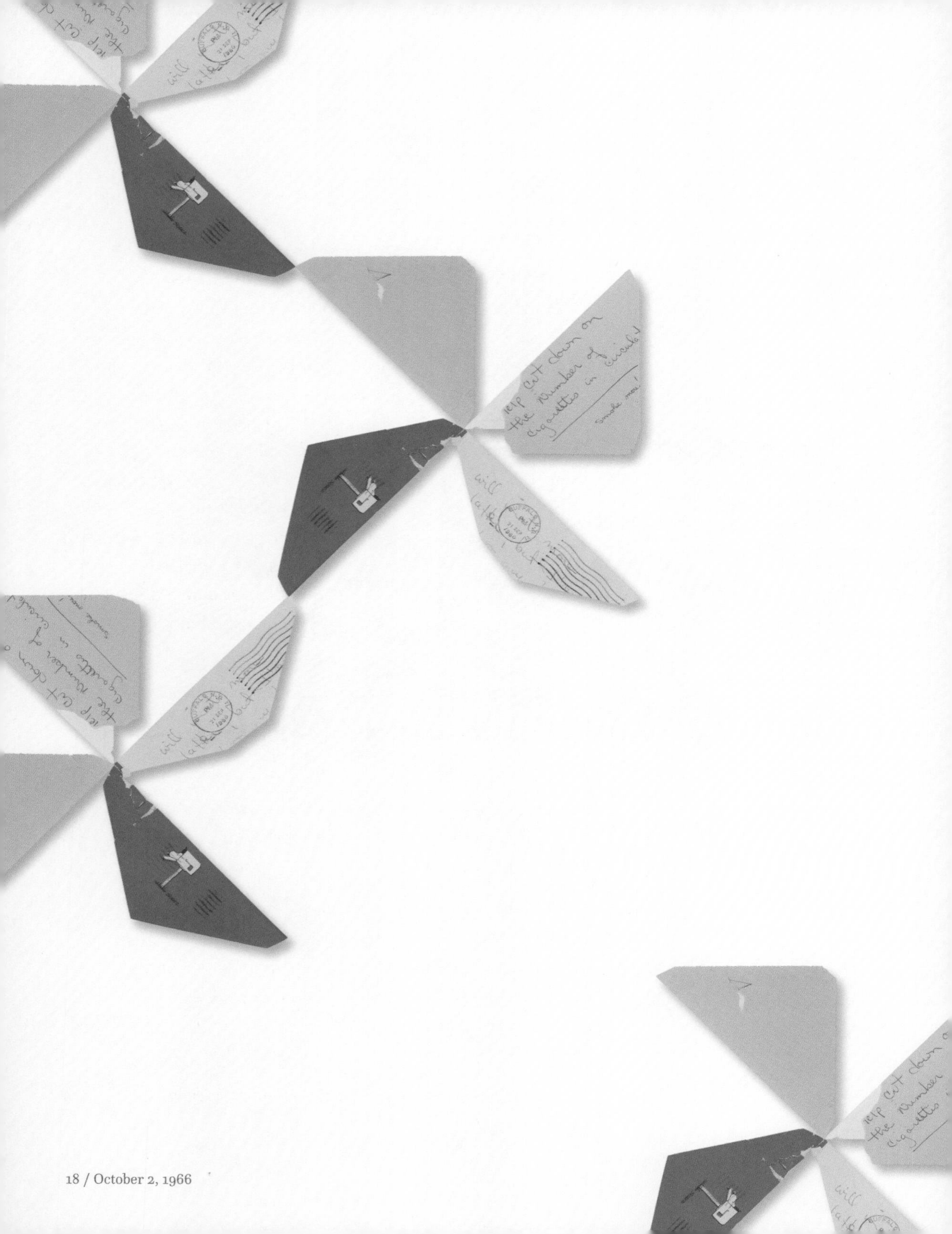
cut down on
the number of
cigarettes in
Smoke mine!
will
BUFFALO

One of the more surprising moments in all of the letters is the mention of my mother writing poetry. Not because it's impossible to imagine my mother writing poetry. Nor is it because I had no idea my mother ever wrote a poem in her life. It isn't unusual for twenty-year-old women to write poems. The affordances poetry offers in helping an adolescent address their angst are innumerable. I have a suspicion that many twenty-year-old women write poems, and do not become poets. What startles me is the thought that my mother was writing poems in the same sorority house where I, years later, also wrote poems. It is a moment of unanticipated serendipity that somehow feels more powerful than coincidence, like the moment I discover poet Denise Levertov's use of the term "crystallization."

In her essay "Some Notes on Organic Form," Levertov uses the term to explain how the poet discovers the form that a poem might take. More important than whether a poet chooses a culturally constructed, predetermined form, say something like a haiku or sestina, or works in free form is understanding the way a poet approaches the relationship between form and content.

Levertov uses the term "crystallization" to describe what happens for the poet who "stands open-mouthed in the temple of life," as he (Levertov's choice of pronoun) opens himself to the experience of the beginnings of a poem, words that "are to be his way in."

Crystallization is a vision, a religious experience. It cannot be forced. It can only be tended. Paid attention. It requires patience, for it is "faithful attention to the experience from the first moment of crystallization that allows those first or forerunning words to rise to the surface: and with the same fidelity of attention the poet, from that moment of being let in to the possibility of the poem, must follow through, letting the experience lead him through the world of the poem, its unique inscape revealing itself as it goes."

The poet must give over, have faith. The poet must let; must allow. Must move beyond vacillation and embrace transubstantiation and the synergistic letting that mystically merges desire and doubt. The lover/poet comes, in this mercurial and miraculous moment, to believe in the beloved's poem/love. There opens an invitation to believe in love as truth; truth not only in but *as* poems.

love

Writing, then, might not only be a way to express one's love. All permutations, actions, and forms of writing—as art, poetry, perhaps even letter reading—Levertov seems to suggest, are apertures for bliss.

is now at the point where
y and Saturday is the now!
g go ——— it was a beautif
special definable way, but ju
, because I got into my pai
nths ——— I've started someth
out well cause I want to b
ing. this little piece of statu
duct of my efforts ——— I
acrylics and want to use new
them ——— this was the te
y news I have to tell you I'll
would be old if I told you on thi
is not working in logical and
t ——— would much
ay what it wants.
ants to say I love y
this idea a whole lot better.
in the process of watching s
movie ——— it isn't that I
o involved that I can't leave
oo much for an independant m
having my troubles in concen
ing ——— sometimes I
I want to say that it become

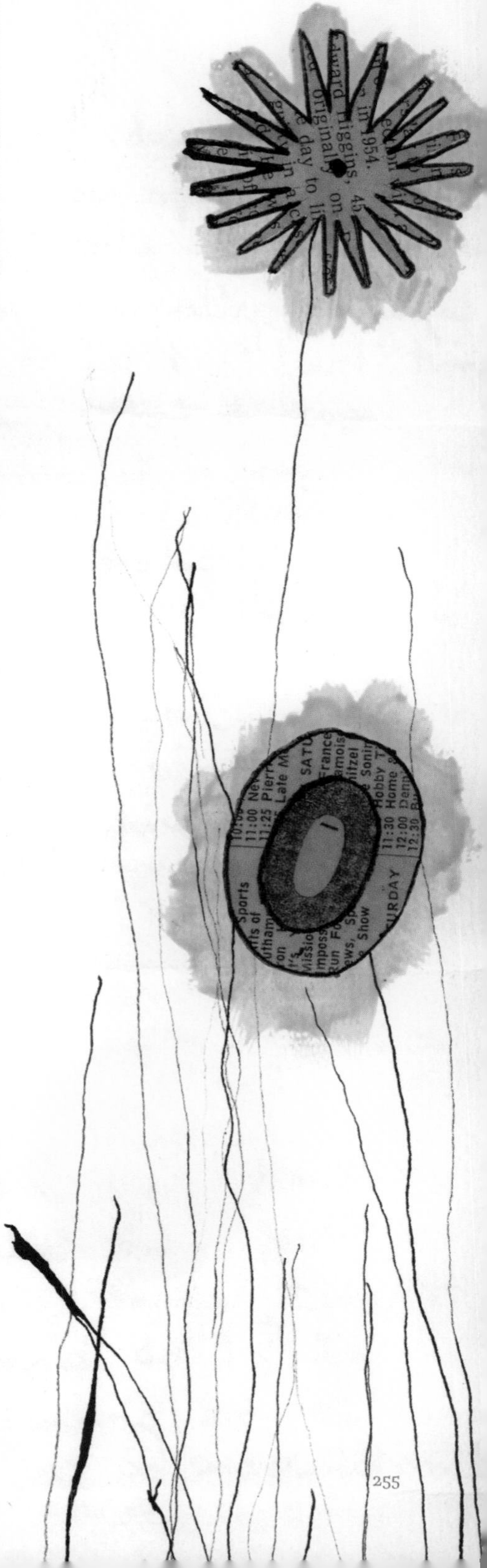

Rejuvenated by his retirement and month-of-making, my father rebounds beyond all expectation. By early January 2007 he's looking good, feeling good, and wanting a new adventure. He asks me about the possibility of taking a course at Columbia College Chicago, where I teach. He tells me he'd like to audit something, something in textiles or art. I ask around and am told there's a special topics course being offered in the spring called Subversive Stitch.

During the semester, my father never talks much about the class other than to say he's enjoying it, that he respects the instructor, that it's energizing to be around young people. He never shows me his work, so I finally ask to see it.

In general, all of my father's work revealed a deep understanding of pattern and color, a seemingly inherent comprehension of the best way to piece together any number of different fabrics, whether they were specifically selected for a project or some odd compilation of whatever he had on hand with which to make do. His compositions, whether prescribed and symmetrical or free form and "crazy," all evidenced a high degree of skill in his ability to make connections between random bits and pieces, all organized into a full-formed piece. Though I fully recognize the style, stitching, and handiwork to be characteristic of my father, this piece of fiber art is like absolutely nothing I'd ever before seen him make.

love

Rather than featuring a central design, the quilt has as its focal point nine page-sized, though not square, pieces of fabric on which he has written a letter to his mother. The pages appear in four rows—two, two, three, two—without adhering to any clear margin, left to right. My eye is initially drawn to the many different bits of fiber art and needlework, patterns and handiwork, that I recognize from my childhood, most notably what appears to be part of the crocheted tablecloth my grandma made, a tablecloth I didn't think still existed. In addition to the bit of tablecloth that occupies a great deal of the upper right-hand corner, there is a range of handmade textiles: fragments of knitted pieces, hardanger and stitched embroidery, tatted and crocheted lace.

While it's easy to see this is a letter, it's also fair to say it isn't necessarily meant to be read. The first two pages are mostly legible, written in black indelible pen, in what I might describe as architectural drafting print transformed by and through particular curves characteristic of my father's usual hand. The letter reveals that the subject of the quilt is not just his mother, but his mother's relationship with color, flowers, needlework; with the ways and places and spaces she and he are the same in their love of making, their connection to art.

The letter begins: "When I first came to her, her world was full of reds, dark greens, crisp whites and a few nautical blues. Sunny yellows spotted for punch." He goes on to talk about the way he sees a series of events—the death of two of her children; my grandfather's father, mother, and sister coming to stay with them; my grandfather's career change from radio and the advent of television to the ministry; multiple moves to increasingly rural locations—as the cause for negatively impacting what I understand as my grandmother's joy. Her love of flowers begins in the maintenance of an outdoor garden. Following one particular move, her interest transitions to the maintenance of African violets, the death of which signals to my father the replacement of vibrant warm colors with a full range of browns appearing in the newest home as paneled walls, cupboards, and wood trim.

As I struggle to read the letter, I notice the many strategies used to obscure the words. Tulle provides a texture reminding me of tea stains. Hand stitching over letters in the same hue as the fabric camouflages a number of words. Frenetic machine stitching in cream-colored thread effectively scratches out many more on the edges and bottom of the last few pages. I'm frustrated by the inability to see the last line of the letter. I want to see how he closes: Love? Love your son? Your son? XOXOX? Simply: George?

When I turn the entire piece over, I can tell he began with a fabric printed with a pattern mimicking a quilt he would have called kitschy, one created by piecing a range of light-colored cotton small-flowered fabrics, patterns, and colors that remind me of the housedresses I saw on my grandma and my nana when I was small. When I hold it up to the light, I can see a second layer of fabric squares in a range of browns, dark greens, yellows, and reds, laid out in a not quite symmetrical way. From the front, on the left, a patch of brown grosgrain ribbon suggests that it is there to cover seams between the squares and provide an aesthetic support in visual resonance with a garden trellis. Though the design was not uniformly applied to the entire textile, it suggests that, before applying the multiple elements of fiber strata, he began in and with the kind of artistic structure and support he both believed in and knew well.

The piece is exquisite because it evidences artistic risk. The very kind of risk, though I would have called him an artist, my father rarely took. It is a risk that works with and for an anticipated other who might be able to find pleasure not only in the satisfying design and pattern and warmth of a quilt, but in the multifaceted, aesthetic crystallization of these "shards of fabric" transpiciously transformed by slivers of thread.

I read the letter-quilt and recognize an epistolary aesthetic as my father writes to his mother. I read it again, and the words of Barthes echo in my mind: "The text you write must prove that it desires me."

Five years after he has died, I come to understand that my father and I were not alike because of our struggle with heterosexual narratives. Rather, our conflict and connection were born from the inner turmoil created by the deepest desire to become artist and writer.

My father's camouflaging of words provides latent clues leading to a second crystallization. In the letter he writes to his mother, I discover a found poem for mine.

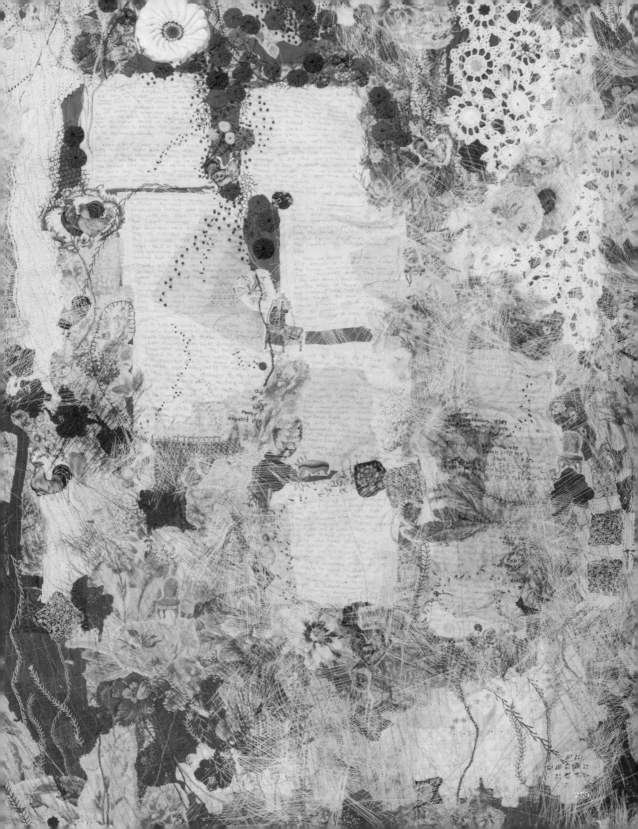

...with my mistake... avoid... that I have... respect for what I... should. I do see they... something about the two of us. And that needs to be taken... the only on this shard of fabric and thread. I spent too many childhood years listening to... speaking of... universality... mouth and saying... of... uniqueness... I just thank my mother... her... and always the... faults... that... childhood... and see... us...

Now, they come

avoid not that

or respect for what I do

that she did, I do see they say

same thing about the two of us

and that needs to be spoken.

If only the shards of this fabric

and thread I spent too many

childhood years listening to

speaking of a universality

and saying nothing of

uniqueness.

Just thank my mother

for trying to speak of her way

colors ended

and needle

she never

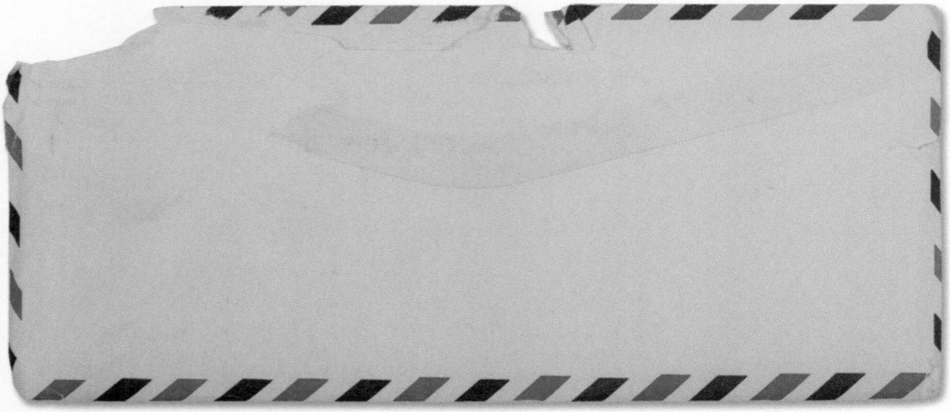

Tricia O'Brien
722 South Forest
Ann Arbor, Michigan

VIA AIR MAIL

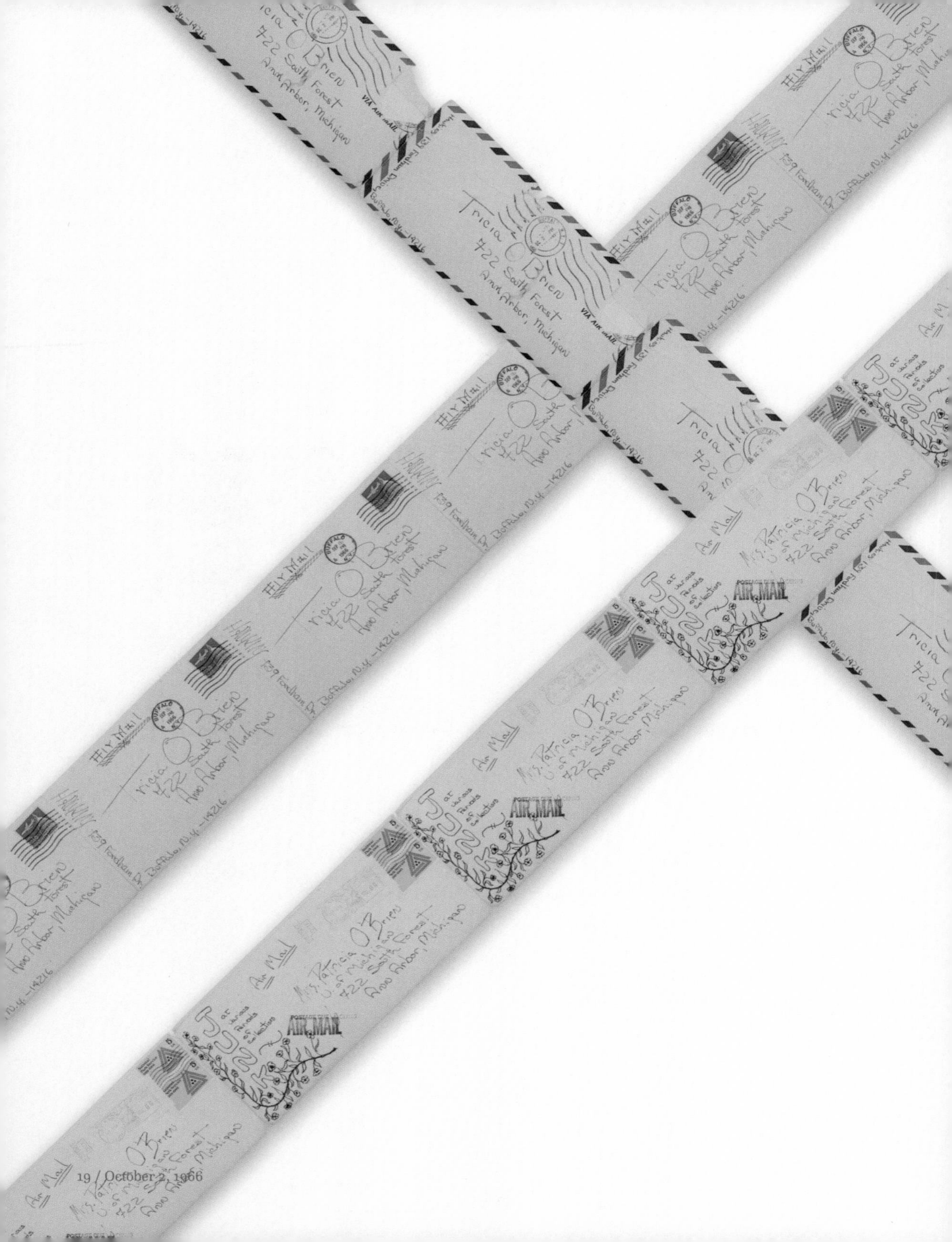
Tricia O'Brien
722 South Forest
Ann Arbor, Michigan
VIA AIR MAIL
FLY MAIL
BUFFALO
139 Fordham Dr. Buffalo, N.Y. 14216
Mrs. Patricia O'Brien
U of Michigan
722 South Forest
Ann Arbor, Michigan
Air Mail
AIR MAIL
JUNK at various Periods of collection

19 / October 2, 1966

"How will the book end?" my mom asked me recently when she was visiting for her birthday. I told her I thought it would be with a letter I wrote to Elvin the Blue, a part of an essay I wrote in November 2014, a Solstice gift for my children the first winter after my divorce.

A stroke of creative genius, Elvin the Blue was a character created by my parents, invented overnight on the occasion of my having snooped around when I was four after finding all of the Christmas presents in the basement, where I knew they would be. I was looking for proof: that the whole Santa thing was made up.

Elvin the Blue was invented to provide answers to my questions: Why were there different Santas at different malls? How could one person possibly, even with magical assistance, get to every house in one night? Why was the wrapping paper different at different houses? Why did all kids not get the same amount and kinds of things?

My parents understood that they weren't going to be successful in getting me to replace one imaginary character with another unless there was evidence of existence. Enter: Letters from Elvin. Tiny blue scrolls of paper written in—wait for it—Elfinese. Of course, Elfinese was not really a different language. More like Braille or Morse, it was a code, a pictorial system of signs standing in for letters of the alphabet. Elvin wrote to me in Elfinese. He also provided the code, so that I could write back.

love

11/20/14

Dear Elvin the Blue—

My first impulse is to open with questions, the kind I imagine myself having written to you when I was a child: How are you? Where are you going to be assigned this year? Do you already know? How many families will you help? Do you like them? How does an elf get chosen to work in houses instead of the workroom? Do you have any brothers or sisters? Or children? If so, where do they work? What's your favorite cookie? Have you ever written any other child (besides me)? If so, when and where and how did you like it (compared to writing to me)?

Yet, to receive answers to these questions is not why I write. I write to let you know what you mean to me, how I regard your existence, why I care about your whereabouts, why I will always wonder, even as I've always known, who and how you are.

To say I regard fondly my years-long every-December letter-writing relationship with you (the magical figure who also brought us Christmas Eve pajamas, sewn by my mother, who understood that if I could see the difference between wrapping papers, I would certainly notice store-bought nightwear) would be an underestimation of dire consequence. Memory of writing to you isn't simply lovely childhood reminiscence, a way to help me recall the love of my parents, my cultural privilege, seasonal joy. This is no exaggeration: You rescued what might have been lost.

Not my innocence. I didn't then and don't now actually believe children are innocent. Not, at any rate, in terms of some starry-eyed purity adults often project onto them in the hopes of preserving something good about themselves. My skepticism regarding Santa precluded the possibility of incorruptibility. My childhood cynicism, my preschool doubt, was no one's doing. Rather, I experience it as an initial indication of my own clairsentience. I knew in my gut, it turns out, as much as I reasoned with my mind, that something about this story—the Santa story in particular—was off.

What you rescued, what may have been then, and I think is always precariously, on the edge of being lost, was/is my belief in self. I *knew* something was up with the whole Santa narrative, so to have it confirmed, though disappointing, actually served to reinforce trust in my own intellectual acumen. It never occurred to me that there could be a story behind the story, something deeper, something more secret, something that required more consideration and thought. If one story had simply replaced another, it's not likely I would have believed that one for long either. But this wasn't all. You were to be and become more than a story. My parents brought you to me, and here's the important part: then I was invited to participate in the creation of you, and by extension myself.

Through years of letter writing, continued at my behest, you became, and survived, and have attained for me relevance beyond measure. You have been shared with my children, and it is my hope that should any be born into existence, you are shared with my grandchildren, too. Because whether they know it or not, in sharing you with them, they will always be sharing part of me, nascent beginnings of my writerly desire.

Don't you see? What I am trying to tell you: You were my first.

It was to you whom I wrote my first letters, writings that were also my first experiments in transferring thought onto the page. You were my first audience, before my mother taught to me the art of the thank-you note. You were my first motivation to actively employ rhetorical strategy in writing. You were the first object of writerly attention, of syntactical affection. You were my first recipient of grammar as passion.

It's been more than thirty-five years since I last wrote you, and I've never forgotten what it felt like that first time, to enter a privately negotiated conversation, to be present with the you—an elf as compositional magic—I created on the page. I can still recall how excruciatingly long it felt, to wait for the code so that I could then translate your original missive to me. When I wrote back to you, composing first in English and then translating into Elfinese. I was aware you were multilingual, and I wanted so to meet you in your home language, inside the confidence you offered me.

Writing to you, I birthed my first markers of identity into being. Became, there, on the page, a person with intention, thoroughly absorbed by the excitement of coming to know myself better, by asking about you.

Relevantly so, there are no letters left to examine as texts. No way to question or double-check what I know to be true: writing to you relieved me of the pressure of my inherent ontological skepticism and opened wide a space for the possibilities of phenomenological desire. Desire not *to know what is,* but to *feel my way toward what can be,* what thoughts and stories and words might, once written on paper, become. Desire to touch and be present with possibility and invention, with internal landscapes, with ideas as stars. Desire for self as artist and creator, for signs as sensation, making and myth. You are, for me, inseparable from my identity as writer: who I am in my love of composing, my longing for language, my aching for form.

And, since there's the possibility this could be my final missive to you, I'll risk redundancy and say, Dearest Elvin, you firsted me: in writing, as writer, as gateway to self. For this, I will be ever-always grateful for you, one of the greatest (most bestest) gifts I've ever received.

From your once-upon-a-time correspondent,
who wrote to you from 14255 Farnsworth Drive (1973–1977),
and 1262 Whittier Road (1978–1981),
when you knew me, as Amy.

With deepest appreciation for you and your creation—

Ames

I wrote to Elvin for six years, well beyond the average childhood boundary created by suspension of disbelief. I didn't write because I thought I had to in order to get presents, or because my parents seemed to need the reassurance, or even because it was tradition, though that made it feel good, too. I wrote Elvin letters because in doing so I found a way to access what I most deeply desired. The feeling I had when I gave myself over to writing. The erotic sensations inextricably linked to how I feel when I write.

I have always been well aware that my mother has not liked my asking about 1966 and her elopement with my father. Even so, she has been patient with my questions; gracious with her answers. And, I have tried, though it may not seem that way to her, to ask as few as possible over the years in order to make sure of a few facts, learn other bits and details that will allow me to more accurately understand and represent events that occurred. It's what they tell you you're supposed to do when writing non-fiction, writing stories that involve other people. You want to know what they were thinking? What it meant? What they were doing? What they were wearing? How they felt? Then ask. I want to be as reliable as I can to the facts. But the actuality here is that the overall story—while it involves, and in some ways revolves around, the history of my parents—is mine.

What isn't and can never be mine is the story my mother tells of the day my parents went to court to finalize their divorce. It's a story I have heard a number of times. It's a story she appears to like to tell.

This is how I rehear the telling of the story in my mother's voice and words:

> Your father hired our business lawyer as his divorce lawyer. He thought your father was where the money was. I thought, piss on you, buddy. So, I had to get my own lawyer. I wanted the tallest lawyer I could find. He was 6'5".

> Well, on the day we go to court it is sunny. We park in the Renaissance Center and walk across the walkway to the Downtown Detroit Courthouse, the one where the Spirit of Detroit statue sits on the corner of Jefferson and Woodward.

> There are only seven people in the room. Me and my lawyer, George and his lawyer, the security guard, reporter, and judge. Half-a-day Hathaway they called him. This is an important part of the story.

> So, we are called to stand in front of the room, and so all four of us— me, my lawyer, George, his lawyer—we walk up and stand in a row. George crosses his arms and turns away from the judge and faces the back of the room. The judge says, "Mr. Hawkins, please face the court."

George refuses to turn around. The judge says, "Mr. Gilbride, will you please get your client to face the court." Bill says, "George, you need to turn around." "I don't see where it says I have to face the court," George tells him. "It's not against the law." "Is he competent?" the judge asks George's lawyer. Bill says, "Yes, he's competent." George yells, his back still turned, you know, "I'm completely competent!" The judge says, "Mr. Hawkins, I will place you in contempt." Bill, he's whispering, but loud like, "George, come on, turn around!" So, finally George turns around, and we get started.

OK, so we start going through it all. The questions are simple. The judge asks: Are there any minor children? No, no. Is there any alimony? No, no. The property settlement has been agreed upon? Yes, yes. It all seems to be going all right. Then, the judge asks, "Do you have any questions?" And George says, you know in that dramatic way of his, "*YES, I DO!*" Now Bill looks at him like, George what the hell? This is supposed to be a done deal, right? So, the judge tells us all, "We will take a fifteen-minute recess while you figure this out. When you come back, tell me where you all are and I'll either grant the divorce or a continuance."

Well, the last thing I want is a continuance, and he's Half-a-day Hathaway so I know I've got one shot at this now. So, as we are walking out, George and his lawyer go to walk one way and my lawyer motions for me to follow him, but I follow George. Bob, my lawyer, tells me, "No we are not going in there," and I tell him, "Uh, yes, I am." George's lawyer tells me and my lawyer we are not supposed to be there. I say, "Are you telling me I can't talk to him?" It's highly irregular, but you know, nothing about this is regular. These two men, they look at me and I look at them, and I walk right by and over to your father.

Your father is on a bench with his arms folded. I look at George's lawyer. I say, "Bill, if I say anything wrong, you'll stop me." Yes, yes, he says. "Bob, if I say anything wrong, you'll stop me, right?" Yes, yes. "Ok then," I said, "George, what do you not understand?" He unfolds

love

his arms and pulls the divorce papers out of his pocket. He's got them on him, see, all folded up. He unfolds them and points to the first place. I don't really remember what it was and he says, "What does this mean?" I tell him. I check with the lawyers. I say, one at a time to each of them, "Is that right, Bill?" Yes. "Is that right, Bob?" Yes. OK, good, good. "George, what else don't you understand?" I say. And we do that twice more. Your father gets up, folds the papers, and puts them back in his pocket, and he says, "OK, we can go back in there now. I understand."

George's lawyer is beet red. He's really pissed at your father. "George," he says, trying to keep his cool, "that's exactly what I told you yesterday."

George looks him square in the eye and says, "Yes, Bill, that's true. I just don't trust you the way I trust her."

We go back in, the judge asks whether your father is satisfied, does he understand. "Yes, your honor." OK, so it's a couple more questions, and we are divorced. My lawyer walks with me back to the parking structure. He is flabbergasted. In disbelief. He is mostly just silent, but I can see it on his face. We are somewhere in that bridge walkway over Jefferson when he turns to me, this huge man, and says, "I've never seen anything like that." He's just amazed, you know, stunned. "I've never met anyone like him."

love

to the point that nothing exists —
not even the room we're in.

     I will love you till the day
I die ——————— this shall be ←
my gift — what ever comes in
the years ——————— It is hard to
say what this world holds for us —
but no one governs my love ———
thus that shall remain constant!..??

          again I say

                 buona notte
               mia amore
                 Giorgio

How will this book end? I don't know.

All I have ever been sure of is how letters—
the best letters—close.

In anticipation of their reopening.

With love as an aperture for an ancestral honoring
of both writer and reader.

With reassurance offering an orifice
of history to both maker and unmaker.

With desire for both artist and poet
to expose legacy's seam.

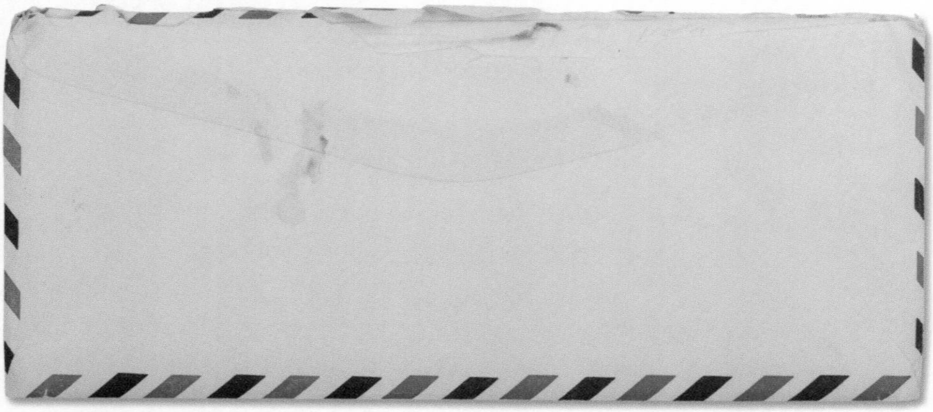

19 / October 2, 1966

BUFFALO
OCT 4
PM
1966
N.Y.
VIA
Tricia O'Brien
722 South Forest
Ann Arbor Michigan

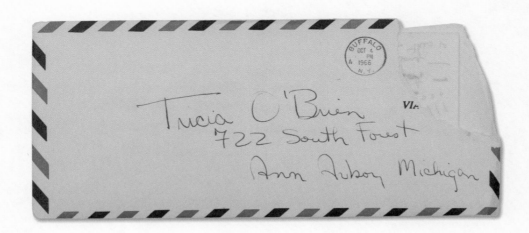

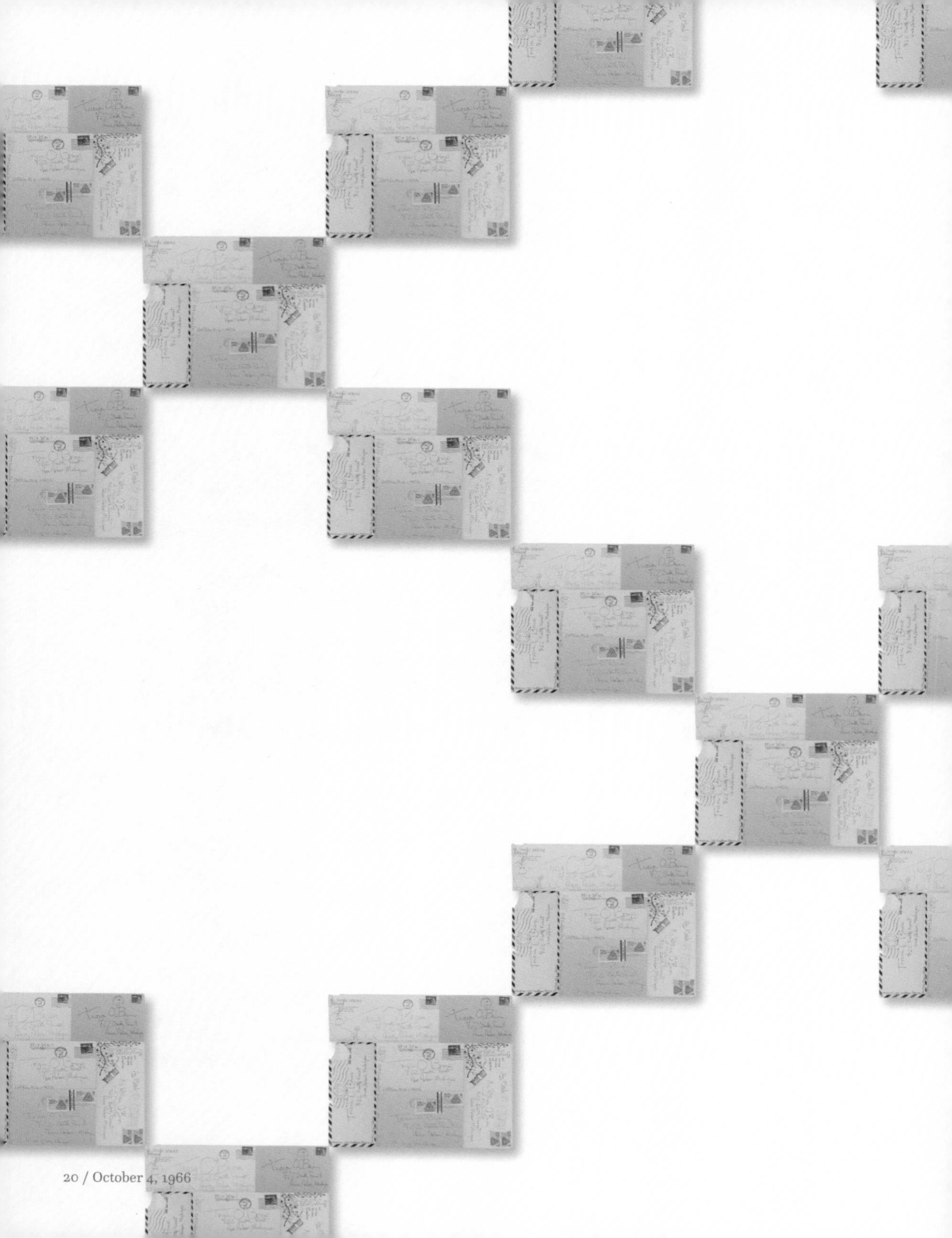

"Here, do either of you want that?" my mother asks, pointing to the celery-green, antiqued chest that I know used to be her mother's. It's upended on its side to make more room for her to move around in this area of the basement. She's sorting. Paring down. Getting rid of things. A few swirly S shapes of foam are stuck to the surface of the lid with glue that my father squirted there years ago to adhere a piece of foam before upholstering it. I notice that the trim is coming off in places, stare at the imprecision in the slops of paint on the edges of the lid, a lack of care indicating that my father knew from the moment he decided to give this chest a makeover that the surface of the lid would be covered. It was being reimagined as a seat. Sentimentality enters. I remember the piece, know that it has always been around, but I can't picture where it lived. I don't remember it being on the first floor. Not in the living room, family room, dining room, or kitchen. Maybe it was in my parents' room? Likely, I decide, it always sat somewhere, as it sits now, in the basement.

The air feels heavy with caution. My brother and I don't want to fight. Especially not in front of my mother about her things.

My brother flips the piece to its rightful position, opens to sees it's a LANE. The inside is cedar and looks absolutely beautiful. He asks the age. Talks about the latch. Asks whether she's got the key. He's once-overing the piece. Perhaps looking to establish its monetary value, perhaps just asking questions because it's what he knows to do.

Usually, when he wants something, his decision is quick. He's hemming and hawing. I really want it, but I wait to see whether he rejects it. He continues to look, ask more questions. It feels like it's all just taking way too long. Finally, I say: "Look, if you actually want it, that's cool. But if you don't personally want it, I do."

"Have it," he says.

"It's yours," my mom says. "Just make sure you take it home this weekend."

I take the chest home and begin the process of stripping the laminate. I look online and find that a solution of vinegar and water will serve to release the thin veneer of black walnut from the cedar planks.

Over the course of the next two days, I make about a dozen trips from my third-floor apartment to the basement every hour or so to repeat the process of drenching the surface and scraping away the loosened veneer. Much of the veneer comes off fairly easily. In places where the adhesive is stubborn, I inadvertently gouge a bit of the wood. I use stripper to remove the paint from the legs and trim, a process that takes another day. Using rotary and belt sanders, I sand each side three times using different grades of grit. I rub linseed oil into the surface of the wood, vacuum out the interior, take the chest upstairs to my bedroom, and place it at the foot of my bed.

It's late spring. I open my newly refinished cedar chest, take my sweaters from the shelves in my closet, most of which have been knitted by my mother, and place them inside.

love

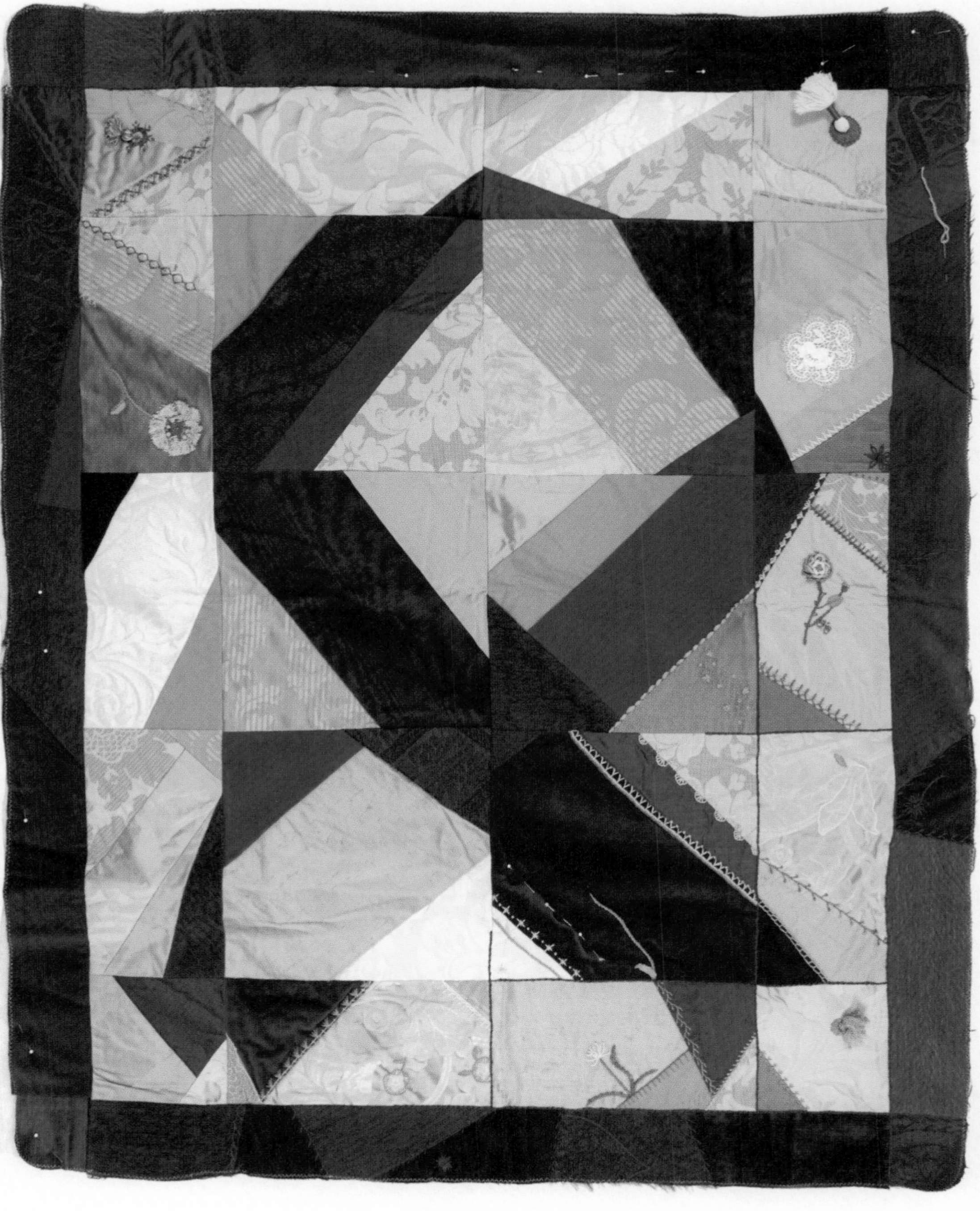

Basements are a peripheral, surprisingly integral part of life in the Midwest. They are the spaces where kids play and laundry is done; where tools are kept, luggage and off-season holiday decorations stored. They are warehouses for items expectant with future action: extra refrigerators and stoves, off-season sporting equipment, and sewing machines. Basements hold tight gun safes and chest freezers, an understanding of hunting as food and tradition rather than safety or sport. They often provide amenities such as televisions, pool tables, bars; the long ago abandoned Nordic Track. Basements serve as practical hope chests, containing shelves full of pots and pans and glasses and dishes parents have wrapped in newspaper, placed into boxes and bins for their children when they, after high school, or college, or that first summer internship, move into a place of their own. Basement decor may be "finished," complete with wall-to-wall carpeting, or "unfinished," providing not even one place to sit; most often they are furnished somewhere in between. Always, basements reassure us that life in the Midwest is meant to be this: abundant, dependable, safe, good.

Basements can also be a means for survival. In a region that experiences brutal weather change, they provide Midwestern homes a pocket of warm air to battle the cold in the winter, subterranean cool in summer's heat. A personal refuge to which people retreat when told by the National Weather Service that there's a tornado watch or, worse yet, a warning.

When they grab their kids, their pets, flashlights, maybe some snacks, descend the stairs, and move to the appropriate wall, the one away from the windows, the one that would be understood to protect them should a twister come through and rip their house from its foundation, leaving nothing more than a mangle of wood and brick or, worse, nothing at all: their home wrenched free the way a kid pops the head off a dandelion in spring, thumb underneath in one clean flick.

Basements can make the present feel like a footnote, the past feel like parentheses. Here we nest in nostalgia, engaging in mundane, repetitive chores such as ironing and folding laundry, often only a few feet away from the irreplaceable objects marking the history of our lives—a wedding dress, old trophies, military gear. Ask a room full of Midwesterners whether they are still friends with the people with whom they went to high school and most everyone will raise their hands. Ask them to keep them raised if they have been friends with those same people since middle school, grade school, kindergarten, and as many as half will still have their arms up by the end. Now ask them, hands still held high, how many of them played with or hung out with those friends in basements, and you'll begin to see. The basement isn't merely a place for holding and storing and waiting. It is a place and space where we, as a region, store food, seek shelter, grow up. It's a starting point for tracing our roots.

If one particular sensation ever found its way into my chest, my fourth chakra, to be precise, and stayed for days and days, a pressure of protest for emotions for which I had no coping skill, in the time before my father died, I hadn't noticed. And the not noticing would not necessarily have been because it wasn't there, or it didn't happen. More likely it was because he was feeling the same thing, in similar ways, in coordinating moments. And so, then there were at least two of us feeling an equivalent pressure due to lack. Each of us shared the burden of not knowing how to feel as we were feeling and ignoring or denying—whichever word makes us more sympathetic characters—the real problem. We had never figured out how to coordinate our bodily vibrations with the energy in this world. In this shared space, we could somehow both relax, despite the urgency of it all.

As my father lay dying in a nursing home bed, I wanted nothing more than for it to be over. I wanted him to die. Not because I had been driving back and forth to the nursing home for days and was tired, or because he was now nothing more than a hollowed-out husk of humanness, or because I wanted nothing more than for his pain to end, though all three of these elements played into my desire. I wanted it to be over because I needed to get on with the story.

Since the day he told me he was HIV+, I anticipated his death. I imagined the deterioration, the possibility of pneumonia, of thrush, of Kaposi sarcoma, of wasting. I waited for these illnesses in the manner that the parents of adult children wait for holidays: expectantly, with a sadness created by hope. Some of these ailments were a part of his experience, others, like neuropathy, necrotic ulcerative periodontitis, and anal cancer, were surprises of the most macabre kind.

When the hospice nurse called me to say that my father was being moved into a nursing home, sixteen years of waiting scrunched up against me in the way that an Oriental rug presses into a vertical wave of wool under the force of an exuberant dog who runs from one end of the house to the other, turning tail in the middle of the Iranian textile, pressing paws forward, accordioning the carpet with relative ease because it's sitting atop a hardwood floor, without a carpet pad. In other words, the worst part, the

love

only actual bad thing about the feeling, was that it made clear that things were, and were going to be, until I could pull them taught again, physically and sensationally out of order. Just as I couldn't know how long it would take for my father to get sick and die, I had no idea how long or what it would take to press that rug smooth again.

I learned that it would take about a year. A cycle of holidays and countless internal bursts of grief connected to nothing. Not memories, not scents, not sights, not love. At least not the way we read about it in Hallmark cards, evidenced in moments of being, or giving, or filling, or inhabiting, or serving, or saving. Moments we crave because they reassure us through human presence. Sometimes, love requires absence, excise, removal, elimination. This, it turns out, is the love my father knew best.

What you want to do, he once told me, while pruning the lilacs against the side of our house, huge plants that had become wildly overgrown from years of neglect, *is to take off far more than seems necessary. Far more than you're comfortable with. The plant may not look so good this year. But next year,* he paused, *next year you'll be in for a real treat.*

In the final section of her book *Three Steps on the Ladder of Writing*, in a final section called "Everything Ends with Flowers," her last thoughts on the School of Roots, Hélène Cixous asserts:

> There are analogous stages in the journey toward the origin, in the return to roots, to what we learned in natural sciences about the constitution of the world. There is passage through the animal state, then through the vegetal state, and so we move away from humankind; from the vegetal we descend into the earth, by the stem, by the root, until we reach what doesn't concern us, although it exists and inscribes itself, which is of the mineral order, although it doesn't hold together since we are aiming toward disassembly, toward decomposition. Perhaps flowers are our last human stage.

P.S. A month after I refinish the chest, I take a nap. It's incredibly rare for me to nap, so I note it in a journal. I also record a dream. I dream about color and lesbian love letters; *Tristam Shandy, Bluets,* and *SWOON.* I see myself opening the lid to the chest in some long-time-from-now. In a room with only a desk and a chair. In a room in which I write. A writing room of my own.

For more than five years the letters have been sitting in a Tyvek envelope in my closet or on a bookshelf.

Now, they need to be returned to the location where they were stored for a majority of the forty-four years before my mother handed them to me. It is the container they know. The one my mother's mother gave to her. One I imagine her indirectly-directly giving to me.

I have no idea whether I'll give the letters, or this chest, to anyone else before I die. I have no idea whether anyone would even want them. But this much I know: They will be saved.

I will save them.

I will be saving them here.

tricia, you married a fool ———— or
so they'll say at many times ————
if I was talented it would be another
thing ———————— but my work shits —
and I never accomplish what I want to...!!!

About the only decent and intelligent
thing I'll ever do in my life or have done —
is the fact that I married you ——— this is
my world ————— this is my dependency
on you ————— just knowing you're there and
can love me when the world seems to
scorn ——— your just being there is going
to make me into something ———

Love you so very much, but have to
run to a class ————————
ciao giorgio

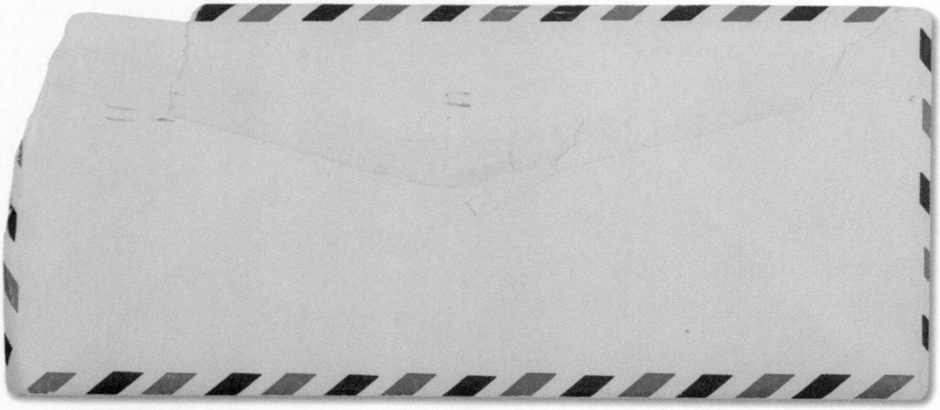

Thank-you Notes

I want to begin by acknowledging that a few passages in this book previously appeared in *The Rumpus, Palaver, The Feminist Wire,* and *Computers and Composition Online.* I am grateful for the support received from Columbia College Chicago, which has come in the form of two Faculty Development Grants, an Institute for the Study of Women and Gender in the Arts and Media Fellowship, and a Sabbatical Leave Award.

I am deeply appreciative of the time I spent writing during residencies at Breadloaf, the Banff Centre, and the Virginia Center for the Creative Arts. Most crucial to this project, and my confidence as a queer writer, were the ten days I spent in Los Angeles at the Writers Retreat for Emerging LGBTQ Voices as a Lambda Literary fellow (a shout-out to all my non-fiction classmates!). The importance of this organization and this time to not only the development of the project but my becoming as a queer writer is nearly impossible to explain.

While the majority of this text was written during a five-year period, parts were first crafted more than a decade ago. It follows that the individuals who have read and provided feedback on some part of this text in its many iterations are numerous. A very, very special thanks to Jen Sammons, Andrea Riley-Mukavets, and Kelli Taylor for reading the initial full draft in its entirety. Your marginal comments were critical to the revision.

Thanks also to Mike Arnold, Samuel Autman, Linda Benjamin, Phil Bratta, Sarah B. Burghauser, Corrine Calice, Katelyn Carlson, Andie Claassen, Arielle Greenberg, Aviya Kushner, Conor Moynihan, and Ellery Washington. Each of you has, at one time or another, been generous with your time in reading and providing feedback on different iterations of this work. Your collective encouragement and demonstrative excitement have been instrumental in bringing this project to fruition. I will be forever grateful to Mary Cappello and Barrie Jean Borich for the support of writerly advice they have over the years offered. The example these women provide me in terms of what it means to *be* a queer writer has been as invaluable as their guidance regarding queer writing and form.

Thanks to M. L. Liebler for his immediate and wholehearted response to my inquiry email. It is no exaggeration to say that I will be forever grateful for all of the amazing folks at Wayne State University Press. Especially, Annie Martin for her undying enthusiasm for this project, Kristin Harpster for overseeing the nuts and bolts of the publication process, and Emily Nowak for all the assistance in figuring out how best to reach the readers of this book.

I am grateful for my brother, Charles B. Hawkins, the only other person on the planet who gets what it means to be the child of our father. I thank my father, George F. Hawkins, not only for writing the letters but for leaving behind enough of himself in a few stray pieces of art to have something of him in addition to my memories. I am indebted to my mother, Patricia E. O'Brien, not just for giving me the letters but for so many other too-numerous-to-name decisions and moments of support over the course of my life that collectively provided me the opportunity to be and become the writer that I am.

Constance, Mikhaila, and Charles: You three were present in every moment I spent writing about what it means to write with and to and for love.

♥ Dearest Jessica, I am eternally, endlessly, ever grateful for your love, support, and gorgeous design of this book. There seems at this moment no other way to say what I want to say than this: Thank you for all you do in helping me be my best me. It is my deepest desire to do/offer/be the same for you. xoxo—A

Sources

Barthes, Roland. *A Lover's Discourse: Fragments*. Translated by Richard Howard. Hill and Wang, 2010.

———. *The Pleasure of the Text*. Translated by Richard Miller. Hill and Wang, 1975.

Birnbach, Lisa, ed. *The Official Preppy Handbook*. Workman, 1980.

Cixous, Hélène. *Three Steps on the Ladder of Writing*. Columbia University Press, 1993.

D'Erasmo, Stacey. *The Art of Intimacy: The Space Between*. Graywolf, 2013.

Derrida, Jacques. *Margins of Philosophy*. Translated by Alan Bass. University of Chicago Press, 1982.

DeSalvo, Louise, and Mitchell A. Leaska, eds. *The Letters of Vita Sackville-West to Virginia Woolf*. William Morrow, 1985.

Flanner, Janet. *Darlinghissima: Letters to a Friend*. Edited by Natalia Danesi Murray. Random House, 1985.

Garfield, Simon. *To the Letter: A Celebration of the Lost Art of Letter Writing*. Gotham, 2014.

Glasgow, Joanne. *Your John: The Love Letters of Radclyffe Hall*. New York University Press, 1997.

Hart, Ellen Louise, and Martha Nell Smith, eds. *Open Me Carefully: Emily Dickinson's Intimate Letters to Susan Huntington Dickinson*. Paris Press, 1998.

Hines, Babbette. *Love Letters, Lost*. Princeton Architectural Press, 2005.

Levertov, Denise. *New and Selected Essays*. New Directions, 1992.

Nicolson, Nigel. *Portrait of a Marriage: Vita Sackville-West and Harold Nicolson*. University of Chicago Press, 1973.

Salamon, Gayle. *Assuming a Body: Transgender and Rhetorics of Materiality*. Columbia University Press, 2010.

Sankovitch, Nina. *Signed, Sealed, Delivered: Discovering the Joys of Letter Writing*. Simon & Schuster, 2014.

Sebranek, Patrick, and Verne Meyer. *Basic English Revisited: A Student Handbook*. Robins Run, 1980.

Stendhal. *Cures for Love*. Translated by Gilbert Sale and Suzanne Sale. Penguin, 1957.

Stewart, Kathleen. *Ordinary Affects*. Duke University Press, 2007.

Stuhlman, Gunther, ed. *A Literate Passion: Letters of Anaïs Nin and Henry Miller, 1932–1953*. Harcourt Brace, 1987.

Woolf, Virginia. *Orlando*. Harcourt Brace, 1956.

About the Author

Ames Hawkins is a creative-critical scholar, educator, and art activist. A multimodal composer who uses writing and art to explore the interstices of alphabetic text, image, and sound, Ames theorizes the power and pleasure of queer(ing) form. Her recent work makes contributions to the larger conversations regarding multimodal composing, socially engaged practice, collaboration, queer literary nonfiction, and creative process as research methodology. Ames's creative-critical scholarship appears across a range of academic and literary publications—both print and online—such as *Pre/Text, Constellations, Palaver Journal, KAIROS, enculturation, Slag Glass City, The Feminist Wire, The Rumpus,* and *Water~Stone Review.* Ames is co-host and co-producer of the scholarly podcast *Masters of Text.* Ames is a Professor in the English and Creative Writing Department at Columbia College Chicago. Her online portfolio can be found at www.ameshawkins.com.

About the Designer

Jessica Jacobs is a scholar, designer, artist, and educator. She is an Associate Professor in the Business and Entrepreneurship Department and coordinator of the Design Management program at Columbia College Chicago. Her online portfolio can be found at www.jessicajacobs.com.